A SOUTH DEVON CARPENTER
IN VICTORIAN LONDON

Published by Meskel Press, 2014
108 Station Road, Liss,
Hampshire GU33 7AQ, UK

Produced by
LifeLines PRESS
2 Washington Villas, Three Leg Cross
East Sussex TN5 7HL
www.lifelinespress.co.uk

Design by Tamsin Carter
Pynto Ltd
www.pynto.com

Printed by Pureprint, Uckfield

Copyright © Crispin Paine, 2014

Crispin Paine asserts his moral right to be identified as the author of the work.

Design copyright © LifeLines Press, 2014

ISBN 978-0-9928777-0-5

All rights reserved. No part of this publication may be reproduced or electronically stored without permission.

A SOUTH DEVON CARPENTER IN VICTORIAN LONDON

The diary of Charles Cleverly Paine

September 1862 – June 1863

CRISPIN PAINE

meskel
press

for Ani

Contents

Introduction 1

The diary 6

Work 10

The South Hams connection 22

Leisure 30

Person 52

Back in Devon 64

What happened later 77

Sources and acknowledgements 80

Afterword 84

References 85

Index 88

Charles Cleverly Paine, 1841-1932, aged 20, in Oddfellows (?) regalia. Ambrotype: R. D. Nelson, 21 George Street, Plymouth, slightly retouched.

INTRODUCTION

In the autumn of 1862 Charles Paine of Kingsbridge in Devon finished his apprenticeship as a carpenter, turned 21, and came into some £200 from the will of his late grandmother. Like so many other young provincial tradespeople for centuries past, he took the opportunity to seek his fortune in London. Two weeks before he left home he began a diary, which still survives in the family. It covers his eight months in London, from 18th September 1862 until 1st June 1863 when he went home to see his dying father, plus a further two months back in Kingsbridge. The aim of this short study is to use the diary to examine the life of a young provincial in London in the middle of the 19th century.

In 1863 Palmerston was Prime Minister and Queen Victoria in her second year of widowhood. The Union was winning the American Civil War, the British were fighting the Asante and the Maori, the French were fighting in Mexico. Richard Owen first described Archaeopterix and Charles Kingsley published *The Water Babies*. Manet exhibited *Le Déjeuner sur l'Herbe* at the Salon des Refusés exhibition in Paris, Dickens was in love with Nelly Ternan, Darwin's *On the Origin of Species* was in its third edition and beginning to make an impact outside the scientific community, and Karl Marx was in the British Museum library working on *Das Kapital*.

The town Charles was leaving was an ancient but tiny seaside market town, with a population of less than 2,000 and falling, though still in a sense the capital of the South Hams, that part of South Devon between Dartmoor and the sea. The woollen industry was long gone, but there were two foundries, 'a manufactory of sheep shears and other agricultural tools,' breweries and 'the usual complement of corn-mills and the many artisans and craftsmen who everywhere provided for local needs'.[1]

> A fine navigable estuary runs inland about five miles, from Salcombe to Kingsbridge...This estuary has also several navigable creeks, branching from either side, and affording the adjacent parishes the means of importing lime, sand, and other manures; and of exporting their produce... Besides many schooners, sloops, barges, and boats, two steamers ply up and down the Estuary; one, the "Kingsbridge Packet," runs to and from Plymouth twice a week; the other which is smaller, called the "Queen," is only used as a river steamer. During the summer months this last, in addition to the regular trips between Kingsbridge and Salcombe, makes frequent excursions to the North and South Sands, near Salcombe; thus affording the inhabitants the benefit of a day's enjoyment at the sea-side, in an easy and inexpensive way.[2]

Kingsbridge was beginning, though, to look the other way, towards the South Devon Railway ten miles to the north, and to discuss a branch line as one possible way of arresting the town's evident decline. Although 'The shops in this place can vie with those of most other small country towns; many of them have plate-glass windows, and all are lighted with gas, which

---

[1] Saville 1998, 210.
[2] Fox 1874, 3, 98. Ferries still run thrice daily between Kingsbridge and Salcombe in the summer.

William Henry Paine, 1798-1863, Charles's father.
Photographer unknown.

was introduced here in 1834'[3]; for the younger generation, it wasn't enough – they were looking to a wider world.

Charles was the only surviving son of William Henry Paine, a 64-year-old plasterer of Fore Street, the town's principal street. (Two doors along lived Charles's future partner George Jordain and future wife Ann Jordain.) Charles had lost his mother to smallpox at the age of six, and had been brought up by his half-sister Mary; he was apprenticed as a carpenter to the builder Samuel Weekes of Church Street.

When he came to move to London, he took digs with Samuel Weekes's daughter Ann and her husband Henry Baker Oldrey. Henry and Ann lived at No. 3 St. Germains Terrace, Westbourne Park Crescent, Paddington. Both were from Kingsbridge, both aged 25, and they had two little girls, Jane and Sarah, (they would go on to have another three children before Ann's premature death in 1866). Henry, whose parents ran the Forces Tavern at Blackawton near Totnes, was a carpenter like Charles. Charles paid 14/6d a week for board and lodging.

---

[3] Fox 1874.

St Germains Terrace was a row of 16 houses, newly built at the eastern end of the road; the whole neighbourhood had only been developed a few years earlier. Substantial three-storey attached houses each had a sunken 'area' in front and, presumably, a basement kitchen[4]. The street was a few minutes walk from Paddington Station, and led directly off the Harrow Road. Once *'When returning to work after dinner I saw the 2nd Horse Guards ride down the Harrow Road. They are a fine body of men, numbering I have been told four hundred strong.'* When one Sunday morning he and a friend had a walk out the Harrow Road, they would have crossed over the lock on the Grand Union Canal, passed the huge 18th century Lock Hospital and Asylum, and out into what was still (just) country – though new streets were already being laid out[5]. One street away from his home was a local shopping centre, and just north of that, alongside the canal, some of the poorest housing in London[6]. Charles's immediate neighbourhood, between canal and railway, was completely cleared in the 1960s and '70s for flats, and the site of Westbourne Park Crescent is now a small park – Westbourne Green – dominated by the Westway flyover.

---

[4] Once when Charles came home unexpectedly to find his landlady's sister occupying his bed *'I tried to get in the kitchen, but was unsuccessful, not wishing to make a disturbance.'*

[5] Stanford's 1864 Map of London.

[6] *The Victoria County History of Middlesex* Vol. 10, 200.

Numbers 21-29 Westbourne Park Crescent in 1956. This was further up the road from St Germains Terrace, which had become numbers 45 to 65. No pictures of that part of the road seem to exist, though it was probably similar to this.
Photo: London Metropolitan Archives, City of London: SC/PHL/01/285 (2385)

The site of St Germain's Terrace on Westbourne Green, in 2013. The whole district was cleared, from the late 1950s for slum clearance and in the 1970s for the construction of the Westway flyover. This was the construction site, and when work was finished it became a public park alongside the flats of the new Warwick Estate.
Photo: Crispin Paine.

THE DIARY

Charles Paine was no Pepys. His diary reveals few intimate moments, and the reader must dig to get a rounded picture of the diarist. Nor does Charles offer any otherwise-unknown historical facts, or even make any direct comment on the great changes taking place in society around him. What his diary does offer, though, is an exceptional picture of how some of the great developments of the mid-nineteenth century impacted on an ambitious 21-year-old from a small town in the West Country.

Its very matter-of-factness is the diary's strength. In the week he moved to London, for example, he displays no excitement or sense of adventure:

> Sunday 14th September 1862: *K. B. Church, rain all day*
>
> Monday: *Making Mallets &c*
>
> Tuesday: *Papering Bed Room for Sister*
>
> Wednesday: *Sharpening tools & preparing to start*
>
> Thursday: *Left Kingsbridge for London 7am arrived at Paddington 9 pm took lodging with H. B. Oldrey 3 St Germans Terrace Paddington*
>
> Friday: *Went to the Crystal Palace and saw Blondin perform on the low rope, with J. Bennett*
>
> Saturday: *Went to the Houses of Parliament, Horse Guards, Westminster Abbey, National Gallery and the London Crystal Palace. Wrote to Father*
>
> Sunday: *Remained at home in the morning, in the Afternoon went to Islington with Mrs. & Mr. H. B. Oldrey took tea with Mr. & Mrs. Thompson*

Much of the diary is such a series of short notes, in an elegant copperplate hand, with very few personal comments. Only occasionally does Charles offer longer, descriptive entries, mostly for big public occasions like the Royal Wedding, visits to the Music Hall, visits to leisure attractions, or significant days out. A few weeks in November, for example, are sparingly recorded:

Sunday 9th November: *Spent the day at home*

10-11-12-13-14-15: Work at 7 Randolph Rd

Saturday 15th: *Went to Covent Garden Opera Saturday evening, saw Love's Triumph*

Sunday 16th: *With W. Bickford we went to Shoreditch Church in the morning, to Sawyer's in the afternoon, and to a church near St James Park in the evening with G. Jordain, Sawyers, Bennett.*

17-18-19-20-21-22: Work at 7 Randolph Road fixing window frames, making sashes &c

Sunday 23rd: *At home*

24-25: Work at 7 Randolph Road

26-27-28-29: Work at 7 Randolph Road

Saturday 29th: *Went to the Alhambra Music Hall with W. Bickford and his friend Mr Heywood, and Mr H. B. Oldrey and wife*

Sunday 30th: *W. B. and I went to Trinity Church in the morning, Westminster Abbey in the afternoon. Took tea at Sawyers with J. Bennett who went with us to St Mary le Strand an high church.*

December 1st: *Work at Randolph Rd.*

2-3-4-5: Work at No 15 Warf putting up brick shed

Saturday 6th: *Work at Randolph Rd.*

A great deal of the diary is devoted to recording his work practice; for example a week in January:

> **Sunday 11th:** *Wet and dismal day, remained at home, S. Weekes called in the evening.*
>
> **Monday:** *Self day and 2 hours making shutters for public house at North Hyde.*
>
> **Tuesday:** *Self day & 2 hours ditto*
>
> **Wednesday:** *Self day & 2 hours making shutters and sashes for ditto*
>
> **Thursday:** *Self 2 hours finishing sashes and shutters for ditto. Self day, H.B.O[ldrey] 8 hours making sash frames for Cottages at North Hyde.*
>
> **Friday:** *Self 2 hours H.B.O. 2 hours making sash frames 10 hours H.B.O. 10 hours Doors*
>
> **Saturday:** *Self 10 H.B.O. 10 Doors*

Charles's diary shows what migration from the provinces meant in practice, how for some young workers self-improvement trumped class-consciousness, what the market for the great new leisure industry was really like, and how the fundamental changes in the building industry, brought by a booming population's need for housing, affected the working life of one of its smaller cogs. Charles Paine was later to become a prosperous businessman with considerable status; the diary hints at his ambition, but holds no revelations about his hopes and aspirations. He had no idea, as far as we can tell, that he was providing a small window into mid-nineteenth century life, its working practices, social life and leisure.

The diary.
Photo: Crispin Paine.

WORK

A typical mid-century figure was the young carpenter and joiner working for a speculative builder, having left the countryside in search of employment.[7]

In 1815 London was already the largest city in the world, but by 1860 it had grown three-fold to reach 3,188,485 souls. Many of these souls were from elsewhere. In 1851, over 38 per cent of Londoners were born somewhere else – the vast majority of them elsewhere in Britain[8]. To house them, street after street of working and middle class housing was built – most of Victorian London that still survives was put up between 1847 and 1879[9].

Much of this dramatic expansion was going on in the area in which Charles lived: Paddington, Maida Vale, Notting Hill, Kensal and so on. Charles seldom had to go far for his work. When looking for a job he *'went around the neighbourhood of what is termed the British Oak'*. The British Oak was a pub a few streets away in Westbourne Park Road (now *The Oak* restaurant), and the 1863 map does indeed show empty land to its west and north, whilst the 1871 map shows it filling with streets. Isobel Watson[10] points out that developers sometimes built a pub first, to give focus to their new estates, and suggests that, for a while at least, these gave their names to new districts.

---

[7] Powell 1996, 89.

[8] *The Proceedings of the Old Bailey, 1674-1913*. http://www.oldbaileyonline.org/static/Population-history-of-london.jsp#a1815-1860

[9] White 2007, 82.

[10] *pers. com.* See Hobhouse 1995, 213.

How was the expansion of London organised? Harold Dyos[11] summarises the different roles involved in development. The landowner granted a lease on the land, usually of 99 years; having taken the lease, the developer then had to raise the finance, make agreements with builders, and somehow secure 'such facilities – roads, drains, water supply, licensed premises, spiritual sustenance – as would make an estate "go", that is to say, be built over without a significant break and get occupied by the right class of tenant.' The builders would both build the houses and find occupiers for them, while others would provide the shops, pubs, churches and so on.

Charles arrived in the middle of a house-building boom which lasted from 1857 to 1868[12]. House-building was still dominated by very small builders who would erect houses by the twos and threes, or at best the dozens. The industry was changing, though, with larger firms beginning to take a larger share, and projects thus becoming bigger. The industry was changing, too, in the way work was organised. The ancient idea of a fair wage for a fair day's work was breaking down; the contract system, long used on government and other big projects, was spreading down to the smallest house-site, and the lower end of the market was becoming dominated by sub-contracting and piecework[13]:

---

[11] 1968, 643.

[12] White 2007, 79.

[13] Satoh 1995, 88-92. Even when workers were paid by time, it was increasingly by the hour rather than the day – the effect was (as the big masters intended) to lower wages, and in the building trade it was particularly pernicious, for it allowed employers to lay off their men as soon as it began to rain. (Postgate 1923, 210)

The houses of speculating builders 'are let to a general contractor, he sublets the work, mostly by the piece, to others, who are usually journeymen, and these sub-contracting journeymen sub-let again to others even lower than themselves.'[14]

Many of these sub-contractors were joiners by trade; Dyos[15] points out the key role of the joiner:

> It became so unremarkable to watch individual building tradesmen taking on general construction that one illustrated alphabet still current in the 1860's could declare that "J was a Joiner and built up a house."

Joinery accounted for about 30% of the work in building a house, so it was easy enough for a joiner to take the initiative in building, sub-contracting or hiring other tradesmen as necessary. This was exactly what Charles was himself to do in Hackney two years later; but in 1862 he had to work for others.

Henry Mayhew's wonderful *Morning Chronicle* articles of 1850 give a picture of the carpentry and joinery trades that was probably still true twelve years later, when Charles came to London. He estimated some 20,000 operative carpenters in London (one of the largest trades), and noted that over three-quarters were from the country. Like Charles, country carpenters tended to come up immediately after having served their apprenticeships, and few ever went home again. In many respects this movement to London was based on out-of-date information, for despite the building boom the trade

---

[14] Mayhew 1850.
[15] Dyos 1968, 651.

was over-manned and wages depressed; 'When they arrive in the metropolis they find to their cost that they can obtain employment only among the speculative builders and petty masters, where but two-thirds of the regular wages of the trade are given.' Mayhew makes much of the 'dissipated habits' of such hands, and their vulnerability to exploitation; he makes much too of the ill effects of piece-work, which encourages journeymen to become middlemen and forces wages down even further. Perhaps he was right, but Charles had been earning $2/8^d$ a day in Kingsbridge; he was earning 5/- a day in London.

To counter this, some one in ten of London carpenters belonged to 'societies', which both fixed rates and provided health and unemployment insurance. There is no evidence Charles belonged to a society[16], though he clearly did belong to what Mayhew called the 'honourable' end of the trade:

> The men belonging to the "honourable" part of the trade are mostly paid by the day – the wages being 5s. for ten hours' work (or sixpence an hour), from six to six, with the allowance of an hour for dinner, and half-an-hour each for breakfast and tea. Sometimes the better class of workmen are paid by the piece, and then the prices are regulated by some trade book, as Skyring's/Carpenters, and others. Generally the operatives object to piece work. Such a mode of payment, they say, induces a man to "scamp" his work.

Charles was fortunate at first in being paid by the day; his first Saturday wage was '6 *days at 5/- per day*' and he noted '*first money earned in London.*' From January 1863 he was obliged

---

[16] The '*Club money and 6^d fine: 5s*' he had paid in August 1862 seems more likely to have been for the Oddfellows.

to accept mostly piecework, and the basic purpose of the diary was to record work done. No doubt this was why carpenters seem to have had a reputation for careful notetaking; as Mrs Merdle remarked in *Little Dorrit* (1855-57) 'you couldn't be more occupied with your day's calculations and combinations... if you were a carpenter.'

An *'Account of work to be done at No. 18 Clifton Gardens'* shows the prices he was getting in February 1863:

Scullery Plate rack &c	14 – 0
Butlers Pantry Cupboard	3 – 0 – 0
Locks & fastenings	2 – 0 – 0
Bath	1 – 4 – 0
Shelves &c in Cupboards	8 – 0
1 Hanging Press 3rd floor	1 – 0 – 0
1 Cupboard in Attics	2 – 0 – 0
1 Hall Table	5 – 0

Unfortunately Charles does not give sufficiently detailed descriptions of the work to compare the prices he was charging with those proposed by *Skyring*.

In larger companies carpenters were divided between 'benchmen' or preparers, who worked in the shop, and fixers, who 'put up the sashes, frames, shutters, doors (sometimes the staircases), skirtings, cupboards, recesses, architraves and mouldings, and lay the floors. The preparers are generally the better workmen', and the fixers often have to work miles away from home. There was, too, a fairly sharp distinction between carpenter and joiner, the latter doing the more highly-skilled and delicate work. Charles was very much a joiner, but in the small workshops he worked in there was little distinction between work in the shop and work on site; he records doing both.

No. 18 Clifton Gardens, Little Venice, where Charles worked throughout February 1863. Photo: Crispin Paine.

Charles reflected, too, the situation one of Mayhew's interviewees from the 'dishonourable' end of the trade described:

> ...those in receipt of £1 [a week] are young men fresh from the country – principally from Devonshire. The wages in the west of England are from 12s. to 15s., and these low wages send a lot of lads to town every year, in the hope of bettering their condition. They mostly obtain work among the speculating builders. I suppose there

are more carpenters from Devonshire and Cornwall than from any other counties in England.

His first work came ten days after he arrived in London: *'Went to work for Mr Kellond for the first time in London at Mansfield House under the firm of Tildesley.'* This was probably Harry Kellond (1811- ?), one of a large family (sometimes Kelland) mainly of carpenters from Slapton, a few miles from Kingsbridge[17], and possibly David Tildesley, a builder from St John's Wood[18]. Charles was mostly working on cupboards, shelves etc. But just a fortnight later *'H. Kellond left to commence building for himself'*.[19] Quite whom Charles was working for after that is not clear, but regular work continued[20], at 5/- a day, at No. 7 Randolph Road, *'houses at North Hyde'*, and No. 18 Clifton Gardens, with one day *'Work at No 15 Wharf, putting up brick shed'*. In February he was doing piecework for Kellond, but being paid on account, generally around £1 10s 0d a week. The work seems to have been a mixture of piecework and daywork, and Charles and Henry Oldrey seem to have been in informal partnership; the diary records Henry's time equally with Charles's.

---

[17] http://listsearches.rootsweb.com/th/read/ENG-DEV-SOUTH-HAMS/2011-11/1322361528

[18] 'The Alexander estate', *Survey of London: volume 42: Kensington Square to Earl's Court* (1986), pp. 168-183. URL: http://www.british-history.ac.uk/report.aspx?compid=50317&strquery=tildesley Date accessed: 23 May 2013

[19] Harry and John Kellond's Willesden Green and Maida Vale building firm went bankrupt twentyseven years later. *London Gazette* 16/2/83.

[20] Plus the occasional odd job: in October *'Removing piano for a Jew: 6^d'*, perhaps at the new Bayswater Synagogue at the end of the road, or perhaps for Joechlar Levy, who was at No. 21 in 1871, next door to a piano-maker.

Essentially they were, for much of their work, acting as contractors:

> 3 January 1863: *Mr H. B. Oldrey tells me he has taken about 30 windows (i.e.) sashes and frames at 6/4 and 72 doors at 2s/6 each*
>
> 2 February 1863: *we agreed for cupboards &c at No. 18 Clifton Gardens, making & fixing £11-12-0.*

No. 7 Randolph Road, Little Venice, for which Charles was making 'circular headed window frames' in October 1862, and continued working on doors and windows throughout November. Photo: Crispin Paine.

and it seems they were employing help; '*Self 6 hours, man 6 hours, about front doors; self 5, man 4 hours, Oldrey 7 hours, about sashes*' is a typical entry in February and March.

On March 16th, though, '*Went to shop in the morning after tools, having finished up all the work at Randolph Road*[21]' and the next day '*I started off to look for a job for the first time, but returned disappointed. I went around the neighbourhood of what is termed the British Oak, called on S. and W. Weekes who are building near there.*' The Weekes were another South Devon family of builders. It was with the elder Samuel Weekes that Charles had served his apprenticeship back in Kingsbridge; back home again in June he '*settled up Father's account with Mr. Weekes. There is now due to Father £23-4-11½. He has charged for every hour I have been absent during my apprenticeship, which I think very overbearing, having worked many hours without receiving any remuneration for it, also charged for the holidays that Master gave me.*' (Charles was good friends, though, with the younger members of the extended family, especially with the girls: Adela Weekes (19), who had a situation in Lloyds in Shoreditch, and Rosa (17), who worked in a large dairy in the Grays Inn Road.)

Charles was walking the streets looking for work for the next week, in the City and '*around Bristol Gardens, Portsdown Place, towards Kilburn*' and elsewhere. He turned down a job in Sydenham, and on the 23rd he was back working for Kellond, building an '*Engine House*' in the brickfield at North Hyde, west of London near today's Heathrow Airport. He stuck it for a week, but '*we have had very uncomfortable lodgings, on account of which, & Kelland [sic] refusing to give me 5/6 per day, I turned up the job and brought home my tools, in hopes of finding a better*

---

[21] Off Clifton Gardens.

job in London.' As an unmarried man with some capital and good expectations he could afford to take risks. Henry Oldrey was not so fortunate: *'H. B. Oldrey gone to N. Hyde to work with a heavy heart, Mrs O. being left alone and daily expecting to be confined. She had the nurse who is a Devonian from Exeter.'* Mayhew had remarked on the strain on married men of having to work miles away from home.

Immediately, though, Charles found work with *'a jobbing master by the name of Way in the Richmond Road'*, making doors and windows in Richmond Mews, at a new Mechanics Institute in

Richmond Road, now Chepstow Road, Notting Hill, where Charles worked for Mr. Way throughout April 1863. Photo: Crispin Paine.

Bolton Road, Notting Hill, and at No. 31 Talbot Terrace[22]. He seems to have stayed with Way for the whole of April and May, until he left London. He must have been valued, since one day he overslept and turned up two hours late, but kept his job.

It was skilled craftwork, but must even so have been monotonous work for ten hours a day, only occasionally enlivened by a bet:

> 5th March 1863: *Self day, man day, making the 16 doors. I was 26 minutes ploughing 10 pair of Styles and 6 hours morticing 16 pair minus 2 head mortices, which were overlooked, and by which I lost a bet of 6^d to 1^d that I would finishing in 6½ hours.*

Incidentally, these timings suggest that this workshop had little machinery, and wood was worked by hand. Carpenters provided their own tools, a major expense. A good set of tools could cost up to £30, and their maintenance some 2s. a week. Charles received his tool-chest from home on Saturday 4th October; he had very probably made it himself early in his apprenticeship. Charles mentions sharpening his tools and making mallets before leaving home[23], but in London mentions tools only a few times: '*...after tea I went into the Edgware Road and bought a small tool basket at Bucks, where I had 6 tools ground*'. He mentions buying a plough by post from Mosely and Son, and in April '*went to Euston Road with Mr C. Foale, Mr Warner and Mr. Ellis by rail. I bought panel saw and foot*

---

[22] Richmond Road is now Chepstow Road, a few minutes walk south of Charles's home; Talbot Terrace must be (part of?) Talbot Road which crosses it, and Richmond Mews is now Shrewsbury Mews, at the top. Bolton Road was the western end of Westbourne Grove, and is now gone.

[23] His steel stamp for stamping his name on the handles of his tools is still in the family.

square at Eyre's', [The panel saw cost 6/-, the foot square 4/-.]; *'making plummett rule'* [a plumb bob.]; *'to Aldersgate Street & bought window marks'*. He kept his tools at the workshop.

Edge-tools Charles clearly had sharpened professionally (good-quality oilstones only became available a generation later[24]), but saws Charles sharpened himself: *'Self ½ day doors, 7 hours sashes & sharpening saws.'* A country carpenter remembered just how skilled a task this still was for the workmen in his father's workshop at the end of Victoria's reign:

> ...every man knew that if he could not sharpen a saw properly work would be twice as laborious and the results only half as good... In method of sharpening each man differed from his mate in the shape and slant he would give to the teeth. I learned from them that teeth should not all be shaped at the same pitch: their method was to file those at the point, or end, at an angle of about 60°, and those at the heel at about 30°. All the other teeth between graduated to these two standards[25].

One can guess that Charles was already thinking of when he might be able to begin building on his own account. In April he bought a good number of 'architectural books'. Since he was paying out weekly, some of these may have been periodicals like *The Builder*, but others were very likely builders' handbooks, of which many were published in the mid-19th century.

---

[24] Rose 1937, 57.
[25] Rose 1937, 53.

The South Hams Connection

Perhaps the most striking aspect of the diary is the enormously strong links Charles retained during his months in London with the South Hams. Despite sharing most aspects of language, culture, faith and ethnicity with the majority of Londoners, he lived a life one might describe as typically immigrant.

We have seen that he lodged with a South Hams family, and worked (initially at least) with a South Hams partner for a South Hams employer. Moreover, the great majority of his friends, and even of the acquaintances he mentions, seem to have been from the South Hams. If this evidence is anything to go by, a considerable proportion of the South Hams's middle-class and skilled working-class families must have seen their sons and daughters move to London, at least temporarily; in London Charles knew children of carpenters, farmers, a wheelwright, a mason, a grocer, a vet, a timber merchant, a malster, a watchmaker, a tailor, a shoemaker, and a saddler, all from the Kingsbridge area.

Moving to London has, of course, also always been a way to hide. One evening Charles met '*R. Crimp (who has altered his name having ran away from his apprenticeship with Mr. Chamberlain, smith[26]), & H. Quick who ran from Mr. Gard, tailor.*'

Charles's closest friend, judging by the number of occasions

---

[26] Mr Chamberlain invented the 'Chamberlain balance plough', ideal for small fields. An example is in the Cookworthy Museum collection in Kingsbridge.

they did things together, was William Bickford (23) who was living in Shacklewell Lane, Kingsland (now generally known as Dalston) in north-east London. He was the son of a Kingsbridge vet, and himself training at the Royal Veterinary College[27]; he went on to practice in Newton Abbot[28].

Charles saw almost as much of John Bennett (30) and Thomas Bennett (26), living in Belvedere Street, now virtually part of the South Bank Centre. This was then a major centre of the building trade: five of the seven largest London building firms had their yards here, with wharves on the river[29]. John was a joiner and Thomas apparently a watchmaker, both from Kingsbridge, but their relationship is unclear.

Another good friend, and one who seems to have been a good influence, encouraging Charles to go to evening classes, was 'Charlie' Foale (20), who came

Charles ('Charly') Foale, 1843-1919. A builder and the brother of Joe Foale, 'celebrated four-in-hand whip' and coach proprietor at the Kings Arms, Kingsbridge. Charly Foale was a close friend of Charles Paine in London.
Photo: Henry Webster, Bayswater, London.

---

[27] *Ex inf.* Director of the Library & Information Services Division, Royal Veterinary College.
[28] His great great granddaughter, Ann Blackler, has kindly confirmed this.
[29] Summerson 1973, 12.

from Blackawton and like Charles became a builder in London, based in Bayswater.

Another Kingsbridge friend was Edmund Bickford (19), the son of John Bickford, grocer of Fore Street. According to his missionary uncle's memoirs, he was 'a young man of strong physique, somewhat above medium height and of dark complexion.'

> When he was nineteen, he attended a Methodist revival service at Kingsbridge with some other lads with the intention of "making fun", but instead the Holy Spirit entered into him, he was converted, and his true purpose in life was revealed[30].

Edmund became a pupil teacher at the Kingsbridge National School and was now at Westminster Training College. Charles called on him there a couple of times. He went out to join his uncle in Australia, where he became a very well known Methodist minister[31]. His relationship with William Bickford is also unclear.

A surprising number of his friends and acquaintances had, like Charles, only just moved up from the South Hams, having still been in Devon – and often still at home – for the 1861 census. Thus Adela and Rosa Weekes had moved up from their parents' house in Church Street, Dodbrooke, in Kingsbridge[32]. Burnett Widger (21) was a tailor living in St John's Wood (who once

---

[30] http://trees.ancestry.co.uk/tree/1636375/person/1419924687/photo/7649c8f3-3509-4a3a-bfaf-22a5b62ca105?src=search.
[31] Bickford 1890.
[32] Dodbrooke is the eastern part of Kingsbridge.

George Bignell Jordain, 1838-1875, later Charles's brother-in-law and business partner.
Photo: A. W. Wilson, De Beauvoir Square, Kingsland, London.

repaired Charles's clothes), but two years earlier was still at home with his father, a 'Malster's Man', in Western Backway, Kingsbridge. Henry Hannaford (26), an Islington wheelwright, had moved up from Ashburton a few years earlier. Joseph Langworthy, with whom Charles went to church one Sunday evening, was probably a 37-year-old farmer's son from East Allington. Charles was already seeing quite a lot of George Jordain, later to become his business partner and brother-in-law. George (25) was the carpenter son of a Kingsbridge timber merchant; in 1863 he was lodging with his elder brother, a Master Mariner, in Sandwich Street in Bloomsbury. Next door to the Jordains in Kingsbridge lived the Bignells; Harry Bignell (20) seems to have been in London with George. Another carpenter in their circle was Edward Tucker (22, of Slapton) and his wife Tillie (20, of Kingsbridge), living in Acton Street, off the Grays Inn Road.

The home of W. Sawyers and Miss L. Sawyers seems to have been something of a centre for Charles's circle. They may well be William (29), a cabinet-maker, and his sister Louisa (32), children of a Kingsbridge carrier, who were living somewhere in Lambeth.

Matilda ('Tillie') Tucker, born 1843, wife of carpenter Edward. They lived in Islington. Photo: unknown photographer of Cross Street, Islington.

Young men and women from South Devon had no doubt been going up to London to seek their fortune for generations. The coming of the railway surely encouraged this, and meant that those who might once have moved to Exeter or Plymouth could now easily be more ambitious. It is worth noting that this was just four years before the vicar of Hambleton famously took on the rich local farmers and organised the migration of their starving labourers' families to northern England[33]. However, we are looking here not at the poor, but at the children of tradespeople and what today would be called professional or skilled-workers' families. They could no doubt, like Charles, afford both the fare and their initial expenses in their new home; some indeed needed college fees and living expenses. As one migrant from Kingsbridge to Australia put it:

> There has not been in the last sixty or seventy years any encouragement to the rising yeomanry to try their fortunes under the tenant and landlord system; or, in the town, for the young mechanics and tradespeople to compete for a position and a respectable living.

---

[33] Hoskins 1954, 99.

Hence it has been a kind of breeding ground for America, and, in later years, for Australia and New Zealand. In London, Lincoln, Exeter, and Plymouth they are also found[34].

Emigration was a tradition of very long standing; Charles's was certainly not the first generation of Kingsbridge carpenters to make their way to London:

> **6th April 1863:** *to the Zoological Gardens, where I met Sawyers and his sister, H. Sinkins, Jordan, H. Bignell and Joe. Lidstone... Went to C. Sinkins who keeps a coffee house in Cumberland Market where we had tea and spent a pleasant evening singing &c, and agreeable conversation with Mr W. Sinkins who is about 84 years of age, a native and for a great many years an inhabitant of Dodbrook. He is a man of wonderful activity and memory, being able to relate things which happened a number of years since. When I told him my name he remembered my great-grandfather of West Alvington, and also my grandfather whom he said married a Cockney.*

Charles H. Sinkins (1811-1906) lived at the Coffee House with his five daughters and his 84-year-old father, William. William Sinkins (1779-?1865), a retired carpenter, had been born in Dodbrooke, Kingsbridge, as had his son. He was right about Charles's grandfather: John Paine (1765-1839) had married 28-year-old Elizabeth Allinson in St. James' Paddington in 1793 – presumably John too had gone to London to better himself.

Another young man of that Napoleonic generation had walked to London in 1800. This was Richard Peek (1782-1867), then an eighteen-year-old grocer from Loddiswell, who become a hugely successful tea merchant. He became High Sheriff of

---

[34] Bickford 1890.

London, and back in Devon a respected philanthropist[35]. His nephew Frank Robinson called on Charles one evening and took him to see a labourer from Kingsbridge in College Street near London Bridge. It was there they met the two runaway apprentices.

There was regular correspondence and exchange of presents with the family, and especially Charles's half-sister, back in Kingsbridge. When he got his tool chest in October, it also contained *'Clothes, pears & apples, a cake from Susan* [Hill], *apple pasty and butter from sister, Hogs Pudding[36] from Mrs Hingston. Letters in chest from sister, Susan, Mr. J. Hayman and from William & Clara Paine'*, and in February *'Received box from sister containing about 50 apples and a good assortment of note paper and envelopes for my purchasing it and valentines.'*

> **19-20th December 1862:** *Made a bonnet box during the evenings of the past week. Sent it to my sister by H. Weekes who is gone home for holiday; it contained bottle of wine for friends and relations, muff for Clara, drum for Fred, Happy Family cards for Willie, ornamental and other sweets to sister.*

The muff cost 4/-, the drum 2/-, Happy Families 1/-, and Mary's sweets 12/10^d. Sending letters and parcels home via acquaintances was clearly common practice:

> **Sunday 31st May 1863:** *in the morn had a walk with C. Foale out the Harrow Road, in the afternoon we walked to Lambeth through the Parks. Met J. & T. Bennett in St James Park, also met Mr. Sawyers*

---

[35] Wikipedia.
[36] A kind of sausage popular in Devon and Cornwall (Wikipedia).

and his sister on Westminster Bridge. Saw G. Lakey at Dammerls [sic] *in Belvedere Rd; he gave me a letter to bring home to his mother for him.*

This may well have been George Lakey (22), a carpenter, writing home to his father James, a shoemaker, and his mother Ann in Kingsbridge. The Damerells – John Damerell carpenter of Kingsbridge and his wife Maria from the next-door village of West Alvington – lived in the same road in Lambeth as the Bennetts.

LEISURE

After a ten-hour working day Charles still apparently had time and energy for an active social life, and went out with friends most weekends, and often on weekday evenings. Though he shows no interest in sport, he did go on long walks through London. For example:

> **26th December 1862:** *Went to Tower of London, Thames Tunnel, Katherine Docks and General Post Office with H. B. O[ldrey] and G. Jordain.*
>
> **19th April 1863:** *met W. Bickford ... we walked ... to Lambeth where we dined, after which we called at Sawyers, from thence we walked ... with Sawyers, Jordan, Thos & John Bennett. We all partook of tea at the Exeter Coffee House, Edgware Rd.*
>
> **19th May 1863:** *C. Foale and I went to Hyde Park to see the people return from the Derby, we came through the Edgware Rd to the Reading Rooms; I lost the sweepstakes, Maccaroni winning and Lord Clifton second*[37].
>
> **31st May 1863:** *walk with C. Foale out the Harrow Rd. In the afternoon we walked to Lambeth through the Parks; met J. & T. Bennett in St James Park, also met Mr Sawyers and his sister on Westminster Bridge. Saw G. Lakey at Dammerls [sic] in Belvedere Road... from there we went to Allington Street... we then walked to Kings Road, Chelsea...*

The Royal Parks played an important part in the lives of these young people. Charles frequently walked in or through Hyde Park, St James's Park and Regent's Park, boating on

---

[37] The famous racehorse Macaroni had won at 10:1 (Wikipedia).

the Serpentine on at least two occasions, and listening to the military bands.

> **25th April 1863:** *walked home via Hyde Park, which walk I thoroughly enjoyed, it being a beautiful clear moonlight evening. The green grass and the trees already clothed in verdure reminds one of the pleasant walks we used to take when at dear old Kingsbridge amongst familiar faces, but here there is this difference – you seldom by chance meet a face you know.*

He did, though, a few weeks later:

> **10th May 1863:** *to Regents Park and heard the band play. It is considered a first class one and the majority of the members were present. We there met Thomas and John Bennett by chance, and it was the more so, on account of there being many thousands of people there, the band being the chief attraction.*

Battersea was clearly Charles's favourite park:

> **3rd May 1863:** *...it is a pleasant place, looking more like a gentleman's lawn than a public park. It is beautifully laid out with flowers shrubs and trees, but the latter are young it only having been opened about 5 years. The ornamental water is very pretty, forming many peninsulas and islands.*

Charles had a lot of friends, most as we have seen from the South Hams. It is striking how relaxed social rules seem to have been in his circle – the girls come across as very independent, while remaining entirely respectable. He doesn't mention it in the diary, but his cash accounts show that just before she started at Lloyds, Charles took Adela Weekes to the Music Hall.

In May:

> Monday 25th May 1863, very fine: *C. Foale and I started for Crystal Palace... went into the Grounds (which are beautifully laid out), where we met Miss S. Moysey, (formerly of Flear) and 2 of her fellow students, she being here at College. We had a pleasant walk with them about the Grounds and through the tunnel to the extinct animal collection; from thence to the rural sports, where I lifted 420lbs and struck a blow of 200 lbs, C. Foale lifting 355 and striking 205 lbs. The Air Balloon ascending then drew our attention, after which we saw the ladies to the train.*

They clearly made an impression, for next day

> *E. Wills[38] calling, I had a walk with him through Westbourne Grove where I met Miss Moysey and her two fellow students whom I saw yesterday at the Crystal Palace. I returned with them to Mrs. Oldrey's, whom she had a desire to see. After taking lunch we went to Hyde Park, had a boat and went on the Serpentine for an hour, where we were joined by C. Foale. We then had a pleasant walk in Kensington Gardens.*

Sarah Moysey (20) was from Flear, near East Allington, and was doing her teacher training at Whitelands College in the Kings Road, today part of Roehampton University. Westbourne Grove was becoming one of London's most prosperous shopping centres[39].

Even a casual pick-up seems possible, though very innocent:

> *we [Charles, and Thomas & John Bennett] walked through St James*

---

[38] Probably Edwin Wills, the 22-year-old carpenter son of William Wills, the builder for whom Charles worked before leaving Kingsbridge.

[39] *The Victoria County History of Middlesex* Vol 10, 201.

and Green Park into Hyde Park, where we fell in with 2 young ladies, one of whom was known to me by sight as she is living near the Institute where I am to work. After having a chat we went home with them, but as it was some distance out of T. and J.B.'s way, they were rather put out, as it was not far for me I did not matter.

Only once is there a hint that the diary might not always be telling the full story: '**9th May 1863**: *I met J. Kellond* [probably Harry's son John], *and afterwards had a little amusement of another kind.*'

Charles friends seem to have been very widely scattered through London – there is no sign of a South Hams ghetto[40]. William Bickford, for example, lived 5½ miles away across north London, which didn't seem to inhibit their regular meeting. Of course, they used buses a lot. Charles and William would meet at The Flower Pot, a bus terminus at the corner of Threadneedle Street and Bishopsgate, where buses from both Paddington and Hackney stopped. When one night he missed the last bus home from The Flower Pot, Charles walked to The Bank and took one from there.

On 10th January 1863 the world's first underground railway opened, from Bishop's Road (Paddington) Station to Farringdon Street. The 38,000 passengers on the first day travelled in gas-lit wooden carriages hauled by steam locomotives. Charles makes nothing of the enormous queues and stations 'crowded with anxious passengers who were admitted in sections', as

---

[40] That said, Whitehead (2001, 95) draws attention to the number of West Country householders around Paddington in the 1881 census.

'Omnibus Life in London', by William Maw Egley, 1859.
Photo: N05779 Digital Image © Tate, London 2013.

The Times put it, but treats it entirely prosaically:

> 10th January 1863: *Metropolitan Underground Railway opened. I rode by it from the terminus in Bishops Road to the terminus Farringdon Street; fares 3rd class 9^d return, & walked from there to the Barbican. Called on Miss C. Gard, gave her hogs pudding and apples, returned to the railway, took first class to Kings Cross Station 4^d, walked to Acton Street, Called at Mr. E. Tucker's: not at home. Again took train to Bishops Road by 2nd class 4^d, & walked home.*

Baker Street Station on the new Metropolitan Railway in 1863. These platforms are virtually unchanged today; in 2013 London Underground celebrated the line's centenary by running a steam train. © TfL from the London Transport Museum 1998.75618.

Thereafter he regularly used the new underground for getting around London – but always noted the fare.

Charles was lucky in arriving in London while the Great London Exposition or International Exhibition was in progress. It was held from 1st May to 1st November 1862, on the site of the present Natural History and Science Museums in South Kensington. It was divided between picture galleries, which occupied three sides of a rectangle on the south side of the site, and the 'Industrial Buildings' and 'Machinery Galleries' to the north. The latter included such large pieces of machinery as parts of Charles Babbage's analytical engine, cotton mills, and marine engines, as well as fabrics, rugs, sculptures, furniture, plates, silver and glasswares, and wallpaper. The exposition also introduced new industrial processes like the Bessemer process for steel manufacture.

Charles went just a week after his arrival and before he had started work:

> Wednesday 21st January 1863: *Went to the International Exhibition and inspected the British Department of Pictures, Architectural Models, Tools, Foreign Woods and Ornaments. What mostly took my attention was the model of Lincoln Cathedral made from 1,000,800 old corks by James Anderton, an agricultural labourer*[41]. *It occupied 10 years of his leisure hours. The size of the model is 10ft 5in long, 7ft 6in wide, 5.9 high – it being about ¼ of an inch to 4 feet scale.*

He went again the following month: '*with W. Bickford went through the Machinery department, also the British and Foreign Picture Galleries, and a large quantity of jewelry and precious stones, amongst which was the Kohinor, property of the Queen, &c. &c.*'

---

[41] See Borman 1868.

One Shilling Day and Half-crown Day at the International Exhibition.
Illustrated London News 1862 pp224-225. Photo: Mary Evans Picture Library.

Exhibition of royal wedding presents at The South Kensington Museum.
Illustrated London News 1863, p393. Photo: Mary Evans Picture Library.

The South Kensington Museum he visited four times; on one occasion to see the exhibition said to have been one of the museum's most successful ever:

> Saturday 25th April 1863, showery: *In the evening C. Foale and I went to the Kensington Museum & saw the wedding presents accepted by their Royal Highnesses the Prince and Princess of Wales which were numerous and very handsome. On account of the great numbers of people wishing to see them, we were from an hour to an hour and half gaining admission, there only being a certain number admitted at once, for which purpose there were 12 barriers erected in the path leading to*

the side entrance, and between each barrier, was the certain number (about 50) for admission at each time, the hinder ones advancing as the front ones passed, by which arrangement there was no crushing as there otherwise would have been. We left the museum about 10ᵐ to 10 and walked home via Hyde Park...

This was one of the three days a week the museum stayed open until 10.00pm, but it was a Thursday, so entry wasn't free that day[42]. On his last visit *'amongst numerous other articles we saw there, was an oil painting (by Cooper) of Hall Sands'* near Salcombe. In fact *Hall Sands, Devonshire*, still in the Victoria and Albert Museum collection, is by William Collins (1788-1847), painted in 1846. Charles's only other recorded museum visit was to the British Museum with John Bennett, but that was to call on Thomas Brockwell Trameer, who was an Attendant First Class in the Department of Printed Books[43], and *'who gave us a kind reception.'* They could have met Marx.

The Crystal Palace he visited on his very first day in London *'and saw Blondin perform on the low rope'*. The Crystal Palace had been moved from South Kensington to Sydenham in 1854, enlarged and rebuilt, and served as a huge visitor attraction. He visited twice more in his first week; he clearly thought the journey worthwhile:

Went to Westminster, from thence to London Bridge by steamer, thence to Crystal Palace by rail, with T. Bennett. Saw Blondin perform on the rope over the transept fountains, the Air Balloon ascent, and all the large fountains playing.

---

[42] Burton 1999, 76.

[43] *Ex inf.* Central Archive, British Museum.

Another visit, particularly to see Sims Reeves, the foremost operatic tenor of the day, he missed because he was late at the rendezvous at the Sawyers' house in Lambeth, but he went yet again with Charlie Foale in May. That was the occasion when they met the student teachers and saw the dinosaur models, which – created only some thirty years after dinosaurs were first discovered – still survive.

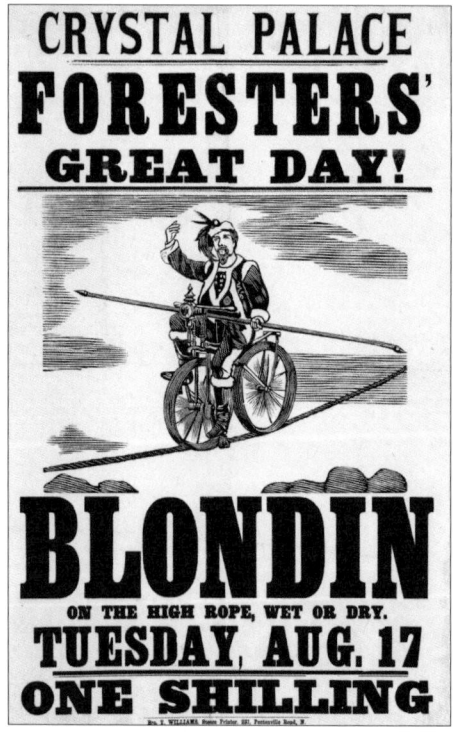

Poster advertising Blondin at Crystal Palace, 1860s. Photo: Museum no. S.71-1981 © Victoria and Albert Museum, London.

Other expeditions with friends were to the Zoo, Madam Tussaud's, Battersea Park, and to Greenwich:

> Sunday 22nd March 1863: *It being a beautiful day and both W.B. and I feeling a desire for a little fresh air, we walked from Kingsland to London Bridge* [a good three miles], *took steamer and left smoaky London for Greenwich, and on landing the first thing that took our attention was an obelisk erected by British subjects to the memory of the intrepid young Bellott, a Lieutenant of the French who lost his life while in search of the Franklin Expedition in the Arctic Regions. We then went into the park, which contains 200 acres, is picturesquely varied by hill and dale. The scenery is beautiful, reminding one of much of dear old Devon. We lay down on the grass it being more like a June than a March day, and saw the ball on the Observatory drop at one PM. The Observatory is 214 feet above the level of the sea. We then walked through the Park to Blackheath, which we crossed, and came down near Railway Station. We then had dinner after which we went to the Hospital which is a very fine building.*

One of his most memorable occasions must have been the entry of Princess Alexandra to London, and the Royal Wedding three days later:

> Saturday 7th March 1863: *went to see the royal entry of the Princess Alexandra of Denmark. I was stationed in Farringdon Street at the bottom of Ludgate Hill, where there was a great crowd and the pressure was so great I was carried off my feet. The procession was very grand: the Lord Mayor, Corporation and Civil Powers escorted the royal carriages from the Bricklayers Arms Station through the Borough, over London Bridge, through Cheapside, Ludgate Hill, Fleet Street to Temple Bar, where they were met by the Citizens of Westminster who escorted them to Hyde Park Corner, where the Volunteers formed double ranks through the park to G. W. R. Station, where the royal party took train to Windsor.*

Tuesday 10th March 1863: ...*being a general holiday and shops closed, the Prince of Wales being this day married to the Princess Alexandra of Denmark, there was a grand illumination throughout the metropolis and it certainly was a very great sight. I met Bickford at the Flower Pot at 5 O'clock; we then went through St Paul's Churchyard, over Blackfriars Bridge. We had tea in the Borough, near where there was an arch erected and illuminated. From thence we crossed over London Bridge which was brilliantly decorated and illuminated, in the City side there was a beautiful Triumphal Arch erected. We then passed through King William Street, Cheapside, saw Mansion House, Royal Exchange, Bank, Post Office, through St Paul's churchyard (the top of which was illuminated with the Electric Light), down Ludgate Hill, at the bottom of which W. Bickford left me to go home to Kingsland. I then pushed my way through Fleet Street to Temple Bar, which was splendidly decorated, gilded, and illuminated, through the Strand, in which Somerset House was well lit up, and in front of Kings College there was a beautiful Transparency illustrating the Prince and Princess kneeling supplicatingly at the feet of Britannia. The next thing of note was at Trafalgar Square, the fountains all playing and the electric lights coloured shining on them, also an electric light from the National Gallery striking the Nelson Monument. The National Gallery was not as good as was expected, through some of the fixings in the early part of the evening taking fire. The next place that called my attention was the Admiralty, also the Board of Trade, both very grand. I then passed through Piccadilly, St James and Pall Mall where the houses of the nobility, public buildings and Club Houses, were beautifully illuminated with all kinds of devises. To Saville Row where (at Poole's the Prince of Wales Tailors) it was considered was the best illumination either public or private in London. It is said the fitting up cost upwards of £2000. From there I passed into Regent Street, which was very grand, crossed Oxford Street, went up Portland Road and took train to Bishop's Road Station. From thence I walked home about 11 o'clock, having taken nearly 6 hours coming from the Borough. The crowd was so great that only 2 rows of carriages and vans were allowed in the main thoroughfares; some of them did not reach home until near day light in the next morning. Their progress was so slow on account of the multitude that those who were fortunate enough to ride could not see quarter of it.*

In the crowds that night was Thomas Hardy (who had been in London only slightly longer than Charles), whose 'waistcoat buttons were torn off and my ribs bent in before I could get into a doorway.' Alexandra had charmed Queen Victoria, despite the queen's conviction that 'The mother's family are bad, the father's foolish'; now she was charming London.

William Holman Hunt (1827-1910): 'London Bridge on the Night of the Marriage of the Prince and Princess of Wales'. Holman Hunt was among the crowd on London Bridge that night and made sketches, though he did not complete this painting until May 1864, retouching it in 1866. Various friends and acquaintances appear, including Thomas Combe in a top hat on the extreme left, arm in arm with the artist himself. Photo: © Ashmolean Museum, University of Oxford; WA1894.4.

Six days later he took Louisa Sawyers to Windsor. Louisa was eleven years older than Charles, so perhaps it wasn't quite a date.

Monday 16th March 1863: *Met Miss Sawyers at 10-20 at G.W.R. Station. We took 2nd Class return to Windsor, where we arrived about 12. The first thing that took our attention was an elaborate Triumphal Arch supported by Corinthian columns. On leaving that we passed through the castle gates and entered the temporary state apartments built for the Prince of Wales's Marriage; it was beautifully fitted up for the occasion. We then passed on to the Chapel Royal which is a noble building with groined ceiling; the walls are well covered with elaborate carving. We stood before the altar where on the 10th the Prince of Wales and the Princess of Denmark were united. Over the altar is a beautiful painted window illustrating the Resurrection of our Saviour. Over the side of the Alter is the stall of the Sovereign, distinguished by a canopy and curtains of purple velvet and gold. We then passed the tombs of Royalty, through the grounds to the round Tower, where we entered after some time waiting, there being rather a crush to get in. On reaching the summit we had a fine view of the surrounding country; it is said 12 counties are to be seen from there, namely Middlesex, Surrey, Berks, Oxford, Buckingham, Hertford, Bedford, Essex, Kent, Sussex, Hants and Wiltshire. On again descending we walked through the grounds and into the Mews, where there was another crush. We there saw all the carriages, harness and horses. The carriages were not as I expected, gaudy, but very neat, plain and good. There was a great number of them. The horses were looking very nice and in excellent condition. Most of them were Greys; amongst them were the Queen's and the late Prince Consort's chargers which they rode to Wimbledon, also the eight small ponies that the Princess Alice drives: they were sent from Sardinia. We then went out and had refreshments, after which we again passed through the Chapel into the grounds, saw the Princess Louisa drive out with her governess. We then had a walk through the town which is very hilly, considering the county is so very level for so* *many miles around. We had a view of Eton College and the long walk from the top of the Round Tower. We left Windsor at 4-30 but did not reach G.W.R. Station until 6.*

The only other occasion he went out of what we would today consider London, was a visit to two ladies in the new Surrey railway town of Redhill, when he *'exchanged portraits with M. M.'* – presumably *carte de visite* photographs.

The Oxford Music Hall in 1875.
Photo: Wikimedia Commons.

Charles was a great enthusiast for Music Halls. Just a week after arriving in London he went to the Oxford Music Hall with Henry Oldrey. He went again a few months later with William Bickford. The Oxford was at Oxford Circus, a large and sumptuous building not yet a year old.

At the end of November he went with William Bickford and his friend Mr Heywood, and Henry and Ann Oldrey to the Alhambra Music Hall. This was on the site of the Odeon Leicester Square and was famous for its sumptuous staging and alluring corps de ballet. The Alhambra was run on classic supper-room lines, with the ground floor filled with tables for food and drink and with the stage presenting a programme of variety and ballet. For a mixed group like Charles's, these rather than the notorious Promenade Bar were no doubt the attractions.

In March he went to Turnhams Music Hall: *'heard Mackney and other celebrities. Saw Barnes the celebrated vaulter turn 61 somersaults from spring board in succession.'* A couple of months later *'went to the Canterbury Hall with C. Foale... I do not consider they have so good a company at the Canterbury as at Turnham. The Tumbling was very good as was also Arthur Loydd* [sic] *as Comic, but Unsworth in his stump oratory is not to be compared to Mackney.'*

Turnhams, named after its proprietor John Turnham, was in the Edgware Road, a short walk from St Germains Terrace. Opened just three months before, it was 'a full-blown music hall, capable of accommodating 4000 persons'; a couple of years later it became the Metropolitan Music Hall. The Canterbury was in Westminster Bridge Road; it was described two years earlier:

> A well-lighted entrance attached to a public-house indicates that we have reached our destination. We proceed up a few stairs, along a passage lined with handsome engravings to a bar, where we pay sixpence if we take a seat in the body of the hall, and ninepence if we

ascend into the gallery. We make our way leisurely along the floor of the hall, which is well lighted, and capable of holding 1500 people. A balcony extends round the room in the form of a horseshoe. At the opposite end to that at which we enter is the platform, on which are placed a grand piano and a harmonium on which the performers play in the intervals when the previous singers have left the stage. The chairman sits just beneath them. It is dull work to him, but there he must sit drinking and smoking cigars from seven to twelve o'clock. The room is crowded, and almost every gentleman has a pipe or a cigar in his mouth. Evidently the majority present are respectable mechanics or small tradesmen with their wives and daughters and sweethearts. Now and then you see a midshipman, or a few fast clerks and warehousemen. Everyone is smoking, and everyone has a glass before him; but the class that come here are economical, and chiefly confine themselves to pipes and porter[44].

E. W. Mackney was a blackface performer of comic songs. Arthur Barnes (1828–1908) was famous for his consecutive somersaults, thrown from a spring-board; he had already performed in America as well as throughout Europe and the UK. Arthur Lloyd (1839-1904) was a popular and immensely successful song-writer, composer, playwright, comedian and performer who had recently moved down from Scotland[45]. James Unsworth was a black American drag-artist who specialised in 'stump oratory', or comic monologues[46].

On other occasions he went to Westons Music Hall and the Alhambra Music Hall, but Charles was at least as keen on

---

[44] Ritchie 1858.
[45] http://www.arthurlloyd.co.uk
[46] Morton 1905.

pantomime. In January he went with Ann Oldrey to see *Little Goody Two Shoes; or, Harlequin and Cock Robin* at the Drury Lane Theatre:

> one of the Transformation scenes was the nave of the International Exhibition with the Majolica Perfumed Fountain; it was a very good representation and a great success. We came home by the underground railway from Faringdon Street in 17 minutes, fares for 3rd class to Bishops Road 3^d each.

This starred the famous Lydia Thompson, who 'fully sustained her well-known reputation' as Little Goody, a much-put-upon village schoolmistress[47]. A month later Charles went with Henry Oldrey to see *Bluff King Hal* at the Marylebone Theatre. In March he went to see the hugely successful American farce *The American Cousin* at the Haymarket Theatre,

> which was very good, Mr Southern as Lord Dundreary and Mr Buckstone as the Yankee taking active parts, concluding with a Comedy entitled the Little Treasure, which was also first rate.

The British actor Edward Askew Sothern played Lord Dundreary, a caricature of a brainless English nobleman, and the play ran for 496 nights.

Only once during the year does Charles seem to have gone to a 'serious' play. That was to the City of London Theatre in Bishopsgate to see the Irish actor Gustavus Vaughan Brooke, recently returned from Australia, in *Henry VII*. He did, too, go to Irish-American composer William Vincent Wallace's opera *Love's Triumph* at Covent Garden.

---

[47] Gänzi 2002, 52.

One January evening he went to the remarkable visitor attraction called The Colosseum, in Regent's Park:

> Saturday 24th January 1863: *In the evening I went to Portland Road by Underground Railway, return ticket 3ᵈ. From thence to the Colosseum, and there saw Decanter Balances and Dissolving Views (which were very good) of Christmas in the Olden Time, accompanied by a description and a few songs appropriate to the season. The next performance was sleight of hand tricks, of which I have seen much better. We next ascended a long flight of steps and had a view of Paris by moonlight in the Panorama, which was very natural. On again descending we saw the Swiss Cottage, glass blowing, and caverns with the large current of water rushing down the rocks reminded one of a truly rustic scene. After taking a good survey we again went into the theatre. There we heard a series of Negro melodies, the Bianci Family 4 children, the youngest a girl about 6 or 7 years old played a Kettle Drum, the next a boy about 8 or 9 violincello and 2 violins played by 2 boys about 10 or 12 years old, played in first rate style and in all manners, dancing, sitting turning somersaults and walking, and concluded by a pantomime of Forty Thieves. I had a look through a telescope (at the corner of Albany Street) at the Moon.*

The Colosseum was built by Decimus Burton in 1824, dominated by a great dome which covered the Panorama of London, painted on an acre of canvas largely by E. T. Parris. Visitors ascended in a 12-person lift to the viewing galleries, which reproduced those on the dome of St Paul's. The daytime London view alternated by mid-century with a nighttime view, a panorama of Lake Thun in Switzerland, and the Panorama of Paris that Charles saw, introduced after the 1848 French revolution.

By mid-century a whole raft of other attractions had been included in the complex, including a sculpture gallery, large conservatories, a Swiss chalet and mountain scenery, a Gothic aviary, model classical ruins, a Stalactite Cavern, an elaborate cyclorama of the Lisbon Earthquake presented in a highly decorated theatre, a mechanical orchestra, and so on. In January 1863, however, the Colosseum was on its last legs – it would close the following year, defeated by the new Music Halls. It was demolished in 1874[48].

The Colosseum's great rival was the Polytechnic, which (at least at times) had greater educational and scientific pretensions. Charles and Charlie went there too:

> Saturday 2nd May 1863: ...in the evening C. Foale and I went to the Polytechnic. Although it is highly spoken of, I think on the whole the Colosseum has the preference. The Spectre Ghost was certainly very good, it is thrown on the stage by some first rate mechanical contrivance of the Magic Lantern; I did not know it from real flesh & blood until it dissolve and reappear, and heard the causes explained. We also saw the diving bell to go down, in which the charge is 1^s/-, which we considered very high as it did not remain down more than a few minutes, and then only a little below the surface. The next performance was the dissolving views, which are very good, but owing to the lengthy preamble given between each screen, made it very tiresome. The singing was also very good.

John Pepper, who invented the Pepper's Ghost illusion, was a lecturer at the Polytechnic; the technique is still used in museums today. At the time it was wildly successful: the Prince

---

[48] Hyde 1988, 84.

and Princess of Wales went to see it a week after Charles and Charlie.

Dancing was another possibility:

> Saturday April 11th 1863: *in the evening went to ~~Caldwells~~ Brendwells Dancing Academy, Circus Street, with Charles Foale of Blackawton. There was about 30 couple & a very respectable company, but nothing very attractive in the young ladies, and the dancing nothing superior. It was very hot the room being low.*

Charles seems a bit confused here: he crossed out 'Caldwell's' and in pencil wrote 'Brendwells'. In fact they must have gone to the dancing academy run by James Bendall, in Circus Street (now Enford Street) off the Marylebone Road[49]. Bendall also sold beer. Caldwells, on the other hand, was a well-known dancing academy (essentially a night-club) in Dean Street, Soho, of which Arthur Munby wrote that year in his diary:[50] 'Caldwell's is one of the few public dancing rooms in London, which is frequented by respectable women and *not* by prostitutes. These think it 'slow': for the 'swells' who pay for their embraces are not to be found there.'

Charlie Foale was keener on dancing than Charles. After their May visit to the Crystal Palace '*I then returning home, C. Foale going to a long Quadrille Part where he wished me very much to accompany him, but it held no attraction for me.*'

---

[49] I owe this to Isobel Watson.
[50] Munby 1972. See also Ritchie 1958, 180.

Person

Charles wrote his diary as a record of events and activities, not with any idea of introspection. It is therefore something of a challenge to discover what he was really like, his character, attitudes and beliefs.

Charles Paine.
Photo: J. Haynes, Kingsbridge.

He was clearly a very ambitious young man, but popular and good to his family. 107 years later his loyal daughter Edith recalled:

> He had a happy nature and keen sense of humour portrayed by the twinkle in his eyes... He was loved and respected by all with whom he came in contact both in business and socially and soon gained valuable friends[51].

---

[51] Pritchard MS.

This seems likely to be right, judging from his full social life. But it seems, too, to have been important to Charles to maintain his social status. The diary contains a few hints of this:

> **14th April 1863:** *in the evening went to the fair held in the fields at Notting Hill. It was a very low concern, although there were a great number of shows, amongst which was a man eating live rats, circus, and performing fish, a quantity of swings, but a very few respectable persons.*[52]

Respectability was presumably signalled by clothing. Charles himself spent little on clothes: he bought a hat in Snow Hill in February, in April he bought *'a felt hat for evenings at McCarthy's Snow Hill, and had my silk one cleaned'*. The next month *'Oldrey and I went to Mr Cove's in the morning and saw some patterns, as I am thinking of having a new suit'*, and indeed he *'Bespoke a light suit of clothes of Mr Cove, for the sum of three pounds seven'* which was delivered two weeks later and the balance paid just before he left London. Otherwise he bought the odd necktie, but most of his expenditure on clothes was on repairs and shoemending.

If he was no great art or music lover, in later life Charles Paine was to be President of the Stoke Newington Chrysanthemum Society, which became the national society[53], and his conservatory his favourite spot. His love of gardens was already showing in 1862. When he left Kingsbridge he arranged for his garden to be looked after by Mr William Port, nurseryman of

---

[52] Perhaps this was connected with the Notting Vale gypsy community. See www.vaguer-ants.org.uk/wp-content/pageflip/upload/TL/timelinechap3.pdf.
[53] Wilkinson 2000, 22.

Bridge Street, and soon after his return home was *'In my Garden weeding and picking gooseberries.'*

Charles admired, and occasionally bought, flowers – presumably for the Oldreys' garden. In his first month he bought hyacinth roots for 1/6^d. In March *'in the evening C. Foale and I had a walk to Baker Street where saw many <u>beautiful</u> Calceolarias and other flowers'*; *'bought 2 Pelargoniums, 1 Thomas Thumb, 1 Heath, 1 Calceolaria at Videons, Maida Hill'* (He spent 3/5^d. John Videon himself had died in January – the business only lasted a few more years). Once he bought a bird, but we sadly hear no more about it.

Though he never mentions going to the pub, he occasionally bought wine, and sometimes cigars. He did enjoy his food, and occasionally notes a meal: duck once or twice, and fish on Good Friday. Among treats, junket seems prominent:

> **Monday 19th January 1863:** *Mrs Atkins came to see Mrs Oldrey this afternoon and brought a bottle of milk with which we made a junket in the evening,*
>
> **Sunday January 25th 1863:** *Went for a walk with Miss Atkins who came on a visit to Mrs Oldrey, had junket for supper.*
>
> **Sunday 29th March 1863:** *in the afternoon went to Tuckers near the Eagle in City Road where I met Whitaway. I remained there to tea had some wrinkles and treacle [sic!] for a treat.*
>
> **Thursday May 14th 1863:** *Spent the evening with Mr C. Foale at his Lodgings, we had a quart junket for supper.*
>
> **Sunday May 24th Whit Sunday, very fine:** *Received box from sister containing fowl, cream, hogs pudding, flowers, gooseberry pies, and 6^d worth of Foale's Biscuits for Mrs Oldrey's infant. C. Foale dined with*

us. Rosa and H. Hannaford called in the afternoon and remained to tea with C. Foale and ourselves. Thomas and John Bennett called in the evening and had some junket and cream with us all, except Rosa, who was obliged to go home early.

Occasional purchases included a crab and '*pod of Brazil nuts: 6ᵈ very dear.*'

One gets the feeling that Charles was a classic working-class conservative. He was certainly a considerable royalist, noting not just the celebrations around the Royal Wedding, but the sight of the Prince of Wales and the Princess Royal of Prussia at the Lyceum Theatre: '*I saw them come out and enter their Carriage*', and once in the Haymarket '*we saw some of the members of royalty, the Princess Alexander* [sic] *& suite, came out of her Majesty's Theatre*', and buying a '*microscopic stereograph of the Queen and Prince Regent: 1/-.*'

In his first few weeks in London Charles joined the Greville House Working Men's Library and Reading Room at nearby Paddington Green (he paid 8ᵈ a month), and in April he and Charlie Foale enrolled in the Elementary Class there. He went to at least eight classes during the following four weeks – '*sometimes having a game of drafts there.*' The Reading Room (as he refers to it) had been going for six years, and had a library of 1,300 books, which in 1863 made 3,500 loans. The club had about 320 members, but only ten paid the extra to attend classes. It seems to have been a lively institution, though: as well as weekly lectures, the club offered a gymnastic class, a Bible class, a band that performed every Saturday evening on Paddington Green, and prizes for essays on *Morals* and *The*

Science of Health (in 1863) and *Sketch of the Reformation in England* and *The British Settlements in India* (in 1864), and had made unsuccessful efforts to acquire a cricket pitch.

> Greville House has for several years exhibited a practical example of the working man's library and reading room, in conjunction with educational classes. As the "Club" feature of such institutions is just now attracting attention, it may be mentioned that coffee is to be had on the premises, and that a smoking-room is provided. The continuous steady work of the classes, the examinations for prizes, and the other educational machinery, prove, that the means of moral and mental improvement are afforded, while the agreeable scenes presented by the soirees of the members, and the pleasure afforded by an occasional lecture or other entertainment of an avowedly amusing character, show that innocent recreation is not forgotten.[54]

The Scheme for Elementary Examinations of the Society of Arts required that:

Lower Grade

1. Every candidate must be examined in the first four rules of Arithmetic, simple and compound.

2. Male candidates must be examined in any two at least, and females in any one at least, of the three following subjects:

   A. A General knowledge of the Gospel History.

   B. The rudiments of English History.

---

[54] *Journal of the Society of Arts* April 1 1864, 320. Available at http://books.google.co.uk/books?id=3bM9AQAAIAAJ&pg=PA320&dq=%22paddington+green%22+%22readin g+room%22&hl=en&sa=X&ei=4-q1UelUzfPSBcPzgNgF&ved=0CDgQ6AEwAA#v= onepage&q=%22paddington%20green%22%20%22reading%20room%22&f=false. I am grateful to Aileen at the Survey of London for this reference.

C. The rudiments of the Geography of England.

3. Female candidates must also be examined in plain needlework.

4. Fairly good writing and spelling, with good reading of a simple narrative, will be required.

5. A satisfactory examination will entitle the candidate to a certificate from the District Union or Local Board.

Higher Grade

1. Every candidate must be examined in Arithmetic, including the Rule of Three, Decimal and Vulgar Fractions.

2. Male candidates must be examined in any two at least, and females in any one at least, of the three following subjects:

   a. The facts of St. John's Gospel and the Acts of the Apostles.

   b. English History from the accession of George I. to the Peace of 1763.

   c. Geography of Great Britain and Ireland.

3. Every female candidate must also show proficiency in needle-work.

4. A fairly good handwriting, spelling, and knowledge of grammar will be required.

5. A satisfactory examination will entitle the candidate to a certificate from the District Union or Local Board[55].

If this seems basic, the Final Examination, (towards which the two Charlies were presumably aiming), was very much more demanding, while weighted towards the useful rather than the purely academic. The Society of Arts' exams were intended for 'mechanics, artisans, labourers, clerks, tradesmen and farmers

---

[55] Programme of examinations for 1865, with a supplement containing the results of the examinations for 1864. *The Journal of the Society of Arts* 13, 677. Available at http://archive.org/stream/jstor-41323792/41323792_djvu.txt.

in a small way of business, apprentices, sons and daughters of tradesmen and farmers, assistants in shops...' The early 1860s were the early years of the Working Men's Clubs, which for two generations provided an alternative to the pub, plus educational and leisure facilities, for working people. Charles was a typical member; one Southampton club's membership at that period was 75% skilled workmen, just over 15% in the building trades.

> Clearly in the fifty years from mid-century to the death of the old Queen, the Working Men's Club movement was an influential force. Although started to encourage the moral regeneration of the working classes, the development of popular education and the growth of the trades union movement as a focus for class solidarity allowed the clubs to be just what the gentlemen's clubs in Pall Mall or St. James Street were, social organisations where men might escape from the daily grind of work, the wife and children, and yet be remarkably safe from the hazards of the Gin-Palaces and the public-houses[56].

We don't know if Charles used the club's library. Quite often he mentions staying at home, perhaps because it was wet, 'reading, writing etc.', but he never says what he was reading. He received 'a book' as a present from Mrs Hingston, bought 'a book' as a present for Willie, and he *'sent Illustrated London News with coloured supplement and Cassells Paper to sister.'* But the only books he mentions buying for himself, apart from occasional guidebooks or museum catalogues, are *'Portraits of 500 Distinguished Persons: 6^d.'* and the architectural books. Did he read novels? Recent publications had included Dickens's *Great Expectations*, Trollope's *Framley Parsonage*, George

---

[56] http://vichist.blogspot.co.uk/2007/05/working-mens-clubs-and-reading.html

Eliot's *Silas Marner* and Mary Braddon's *Lady Audley's Secret*.

Just after moving to London he received a paternal letter, which survives, with the admonition: 'I have sent your Bible in hope the Lord will instill in your mind the proper and enlightened use of it I hope you will not forget the Savings Bank Bank [sic: but?] make the Effort to use regularly either weekly or Monthly and when you begin you will find it more pleasure to Continue.' A month later Charles's father wrote again: 'you have every Evening many Hours and at your commencement [?] might be beneficially employed I hope the Lord will Direct your path and Do not think because you are earning good Wages that there is not an account to be given for the bestowal of it in a proper and judicious manner I don't hear of your having found a Weekly Depo [?] for Savings.' For Charles's father, at least, the primary religious duty seems to be the proper stewardship of time and money. He passes on, though, a message from 'Dear Mr Popplestone[57] and he desired me through the blessing of the Lord to be kindly remembered to you, and tell him for me to Keep the Sabbath Day an Holy Day and may the Lord bless him. I promised him to do so. He is a Happy Christian.'

Judging by his assiduous diary keeping and weekly accounts, as well as his business success in later life, Charles followed his father's precept; his Sabbath-keeping was perhaps less consistent. In London Charles would occasionally go to church, and his devotion was sincere, if perhaps conventional. In his last letter to his father he said:

---

[57] Perhaps Henry Popplestone, 71, tailor of Church Street.

I am happy to hear that you are happy and waiting the Lords time, believing on the Lord Jesus Christ who suffered and died for us all, that we through his death, believing on him, might be saved from death eternal[58].

On his second Sunday in London, and twice later, he went to 'The Trinity Church': presumably Holy Trinity Bishops Road, Paddington, (built 1846 by Thomas Cundy, closed in 1971 and demolished in 1984.) During November he and William Bickford sampled various central London churches: Temple Church, St Botolph's Bishopsgate, St Mary le Strand, Shoreditch Church and 'a church near St. James Park'. Once a long walk with friends took them to *'Regents Circus near where we went to church, but the heat being so oppressive we came out after the reading of the Lessons and soon separated, each for his own home.'*

A more interesting Sunday must have been when in the morning he attended *'a Pusaite church'* [sic] in Kingsland, and in the evening Mr. Myers' church there. The Puseyite church was surely the church of St. Matthias, Stoke Newington, built by the great if maverick architect William Butterfield in 1851-54[59]. Sadly, it was gutted in the war, though it is still High Church and still a wonderful building. Which was Mr. Myers' church is not clear: the minister of Kingsland Independent Chapel was Dr. Aveling.

---

[58] See St. John's Gospel 5: 24.
[59] Butterfield was designing it at the same time as the far better known All Saints Margaret Street. Anson (1960, 200) illustrates the sanctuary decorated for Christmas about 1870, perhaps much as Charles would have seen it in December 1862.

The only comments Charles makes on any church are on a sermon: *'in the evening we went to St. Andrews Church, Holborn Hill, & heard an excellent sermon on these words, 'Almost persuaded to be a Christian.'* One Sunday evening in October he went to hear the famous evangelist Charles Spurgeon at the Metropolitan Tabernacle at the Elephant and Castle. This enormous Baptist church had been built a year before: it could hold 6,500 people. Spurgeon published most of his sermons, and the one Charles heard that evening can be read a century and a half later on the web[60]; it was on the text *'The name of the Lord is a strong tower: the righteous runneth into it, and is safe'* (Proverbs 18:10).

In Kingsbridge he went either to Church or to Chapel every week. On July 5th *'I am this day 22 years old. Went to Chapel in the morning; took tea with Miss E. Crimp; went to Church in the evening.'* The Independent Chapel, now the Evangelical Church, was just across the road from his father's house; it had been rebuilt five years earlier in an old-fashioned nonconformist style.

Charles sounds, though, more of a Church conservative than a Chapel radical. One of Mayhew's interviewees suggested 'Joiners' work is noisy, and they can't talk when carrying it on, and that may account for joiners not being such politicians or thinkers as shoemakers or tailors'; indeed Charles showed little interest in politics, Parliamentary or otherwise. He once happened upon *'a monster Garibaldian meeting'* in Hyde Park

---

[60] www.biblebb.com/files/spurgeon/0491.htm

in October, but he reveals no interest in the London Trades Council which was trying to organise a working-class welcome for the proposed visit by Garibaldi, nor in any of the other great issues of the day, for example support for the North in the American Civil War. Only once does he show any interest in public affairs[61], and then one suspects that it was again Charlie Foale's influence:

> **8th May 1863:** *C. Foale and I went to a working men's meeting in Westbourne Grove held in favour of the Public House Sunday Closing Bill, Lord Radstock in the chair.*

The Sunday Closing Bill, promoted by the Lords Day Observance Society and supported by many manufacturers, was vehemently opposed by many working people. (Lord Radstock, Granville Waldegrave (1833-1913), after experiencing a religious conversion while recovering from fever in the Crimea, devoted his time and wealth to philanthropic and evangelistic work.) The Bill was heavily defeated. Did the two Charlies attend the meeting because they supported the Bill? Was Charles trying to obey Mr Popplestone's injunction? If so he was hardly consistent. One Sunday he noted:

> **10th May 1863:** *some short time since a few biased individuals (compared with the many thousands who enjoy it) tried their utmost to put a stop to the bands playing in any of the parks on the Sabbath, but were defeated.*

More surprising, perhaps, is that his diary makes no mention

---

[61] Though in November he does subscribe to a 'Lancashire distress' appeal. This was a response to the Lancashire Cotton Famine, a very serious crisis caused by the blocking of cotton imports from the southern American States.

of the politics that in the early 1860s were swirling around the building trades. Just two years earlier the lockout imposed by the big master-builders of London, 'a body of men traditionally tyrannous and autocratic'[62], had temporarily halted the campaign for a nine-hour day, but given a huge fillip to trades-unionism and more widely to working-class organisation. The very moderate Amalgamated Society of Carpenters and Joiners was founded in London in 1860, the rival (and more militant) General Union of Carpenters and Joiners was revived in 1862.

The new unionism was marked by caution and moderation: 'Temperance, self-education, chastity, self-restraint and hard work were pressed upon their followers'[63]. What little evidence we have suggests that Charles shared just this ethos, which so contrasted with the class-war militancy of the previous generation. But there is no indication that he ever joined a union.

---

[62] Postgate 1923, 171.
[63] Postgate 1923, 192.

Back in Devon

On Saturday 30th of May Charles got another worrying letter from his half-sister Mary, reporting that their father was still very ill. So on Monday, *'Packed my things and got ready for starting home. Went down to Bishop Road, bought whip for Fred and work box for Clara, also some oranges to eat on the passage. Had cab to take my box to station.'*

Paddington Station, painted in 1862 by William Powell Frith. Not only was it from this station (then still called Bishop Road) that Charles travelled to and from Devon and to and from work at North Hyde, but on the night he came home to find Adela Weekes occupying his bed, 'I went down to G.W.R. station. I remained there until past 4am, I then went to a Coffee House where I remained until 7-30am.'
Photo: © Royal Holloway College.

The journey home turned into something of a marathon. Firstly, he had agreed to take the Oldreys' four-year-old daughter Janie to her grandmother's – presumably because her mother was about to have another baby, and her father away working. The elder Jane Oldrey (43) ran the Forces Tavern at Blackawton, a remote crossroads pub in the lush and beautiful countryside between Totnes and Kingsbridge.

> *her father came as far as Southall with us, he being at North Hyde to work. Janie was a very good girl all the way; we arrived at Exeter 6-30 where we waited upwards of an hour, arriving at Totnes 8-7, where we expected to find a conveyance to take the little girl to Forces, but as there was none I hired one and went with her, her grandmother paying for it and I paid the turnpike. We met S. Wakeham on the Road coming to meet me, with a pony for me to ride, after having been to Forces to see if I was there; we got to Forces about 11 O'clock. On the road we had a good view of the eclipse of the moon, it being total during the time we were at Forces, where we (J.E [sic], Sam. W. and I) had some tea and boiled eggs, one of which was not edible. By the time we left the moon was again making her appearance. As I had been riding all day I preferred walking, and walked from Blackawton Forces home, a distance of about 8 miles, where we arrived about ½ past one.*

The Forces Tavern, Blackawton, Devon, in 2013. Photo: Crispin Paine.

Once in Kingsbridge he went straight to Mary's house in Mill Street, at the bottom of the town just behind the Quay. Mary had lost her husband three years earlier, and was struggling[64] to bring up her three children, aged nine, seven and five, and to run a grocer's shop. She wasn't there, so Charles went back up Fore Street some hundred yards to his father's house on the corner of Baptist Lane, where Mary was waiting for him. *'I found Father in bed much altered for the worse since I left home, he was suffering much pain in his back and very weak.*'

It was now the middle of the night; Charles had been travelling for some fifteen hours, and had just walked eight miles. It is scarcely surprising that *'after I had been in his room a short time I felt very faint, from traveling excitement and the heat of the room, and had difficulty in leaving the room and getting down stairs.'* But *'I soon got the better of it, and did good justice to some sausages which Mrs Harley* [his father's housekeeper] *and my sister had cooked for me. After dispatching them I accompanied my sister home, and remained there talking with her until daylight, when I went home and turned into bed.'*

During the two months in Kingsbridge that the diary now describes, Charles divided his time between looking after his father, catching up with relatives, a number of jolly excursions with friends, and doing jobs for the family.

His father was indeed very ill, and was to die just a few months

---

[64] According to reminiscences of Charles's daughter Janet, quoted in Michael Paine's 1982 family notes.

Clarenda ('Clara') Paine, 1856-1930, Charles's half-niece.
Photo: J. Ash, Kingsbridge.

Mary Paine, 1831-1909, Charles's half-sister. Though this photo is identified as Mary in Charles's album, she is dressed in the style of the 1890s, when she would have been in her 60s and was living in London.
Photo: Mrs Haynes, Kingsbridge.

Charles Frederick Paine, 1858-1947, Charles's half-nephew.
Photo: Pound, Kingsbridge.

Susan Hill, 1804-1868, a friend of Charles's mother.
Photo: J. Haynes, Kingsbridge.

later. His doctor, Dr. Ford, diagnosed 'diseased kidneys'; but the only treatment mentioned was '*12 leeches applied to his back after he had a warm bath*'; the next morning he was '*a little easier but very weak.*' It has been suggested he was suffering from kidney stones. Charles tried to make his life easier and more interesting by installing a handrail on his stairs, and '*Got Father up in my garden with a deal of trouble to him.*' He also spent a good deal of time going through his father's papers and putting his affairs in order, with much help from William Wills, the builder from Flora Place, Ebrington Street, for whom he had been working before he left Kingsbridge. He even '*received forty pounds from him on ac^t for father.*'

Charles caught up, too, with other family and friends. He went out (a fifteen-minute walk from town) to West Alvington to visit Uncle John, like his brother a plasterer, and step-aunt Mary. He ate a number of times at Susan Hill's. She had been a friend of Charles's mother, and clearly had a soft spot for Charles to whom she wrote and sent presents when he was in London, and whom she made her principal beneficiary and executor[65].

---

[65] Will dated 17.2.1864.

She was housekeeper at Butville House (now Kahala Court care home), a prominent Regency house overlooking the estuary, while the owners Mr. and Mrs. Hawkins were away.

One day he combined a shopping trip for his sister with visits to cousins in Plymouth:

> **3rd/4th July 1863:** *I went to Plymouth by midday coach to station & train, to see my friends and buy things for my sister... I had tea at Aunt Jane Ellis, after which I went to my cousin's John Ellis with cousin Selina Ellis; in the evening went to the Mechanics Institute, with John and his wife, and heard Templeton's African Opera Troupe.* They gave a very good evening's entertainment [in April this black-face minstrel group had been in Halifax] *after which I went home with John to supper, when his wife kindly offered to make up a bed for me on the sofa, which I accepted. Had breakfast with John, I then went and did what business I had to do and saw whom I wanted, then returned to Aunt's and had dinner, after which I went home by steamer. It was a delightful voyage, the sea being very calm.*

The closest railway station to Kingsbridge was near the village of Wrangaton, ten miles to the north. Foale's or Tucker's ran a number of coaches

Jane Lome Ellis, 1806-1889, Charles's aunt. She was the widow of a mason, worked as a dressmaker, and lived in Friary Green, Plymouth, with her daughter and two sons.

every day to meet trains. Kingsbridge Road Station, as it was then called (later Wrangaton Station), was almost at the foot of Dartmoor; indeed, it is said to feature in *The Hound of the Baskervilles*.

The next day, Sunday, was Charles's birthday; he had tea with Miss E. Crimp – perhaps Emma Crimp, a twenty-five-year-old dressmaker of Mill Street – and went to church.

Charles records just one job in his first four months back home: a new shopfront for Samuel Perrott's saddlery shop[66], which his father owned; this was at the front of his father's house, facing Fore Street. Charles did the basic work in William Wills's workshop, and the whole job took 'at intervals' fifteen days, but he was proud of the result: *'On the 3rd of July I finished the shop front at Perrotts for Father, which is a great improvement to the house and town.'* Ever provident, he advertised the old window ('For Sale: a Bargain') in the next week's *Kingsbridge Gazette*.

He also helped his sister with her Refreshment Booth at the Oddfellows Fete, putting up a stall, and going to Plymouth to buy supplies. The fete took place on a field behind Boxhill, a big house now called Dodbrooke Manor. The event seems to have been quite significant in the district; the log-book for the National School at Stokenham, six miles from the town, records 'Rainy. Usual progress. On this day there is an Odd Fellows Fete at Kingsbridge in Aid of Funds of Life Boat Society

---

[66] Perrotts were apparently not only saddlers. In 1871 a fishing rod made by Perrott of Kingsbridge landed a three-foot alligator in Guyana (Pitman 1872).

Perrott's shop, Fore Street, Kingsbridge, perhaps about 1900. The Perrotts ran it from 1861 until 1977. Photo: Cookworthy Museum P04996.

'Alan's Apple', Fore Street, Kingsbridge, in 2013. This was Perrott the saddler's shop, in front of his father's house, for which Charles made a new window in June 1863. It seems quite possible that part of the present window is Charles's work.
Photo: Crispin Paine.

– many children there with their parents.'[67] Let's hope they all patronised the refreshment tent.

Charles went on a whole series of trips that summer:

> **Wednesday 17th June 1863:** *in the evening went on the water in a boat with Miss Anning, Miss Jeffrey, Misses Mary, Jane, Clara and Leah Cranch, Miss Hyne, S. Perrott, J. Brown, Alf, and Ed. Cranch*
>
> **Wednesday 8th July 1863:** *in the afternoon I went to Salcombe with Mr J. Cranch, Misses R Foale, M. J. & E. Cranch.*
>
> *On the 16th* [**Thursday**] *I went the Excursion trip of the Kingsbridge Packet to Plymouth, in company with Miss Anning, Miss M. J. Cranch, S. Perrott & Mr J. Cranch. We dined at Mechams in Bedford Street, then took bus to Devonport, went to the bazaar held in and in behalf of the new hospital. After hearing the Marine and other bands play and seeing the flower show and as much else as could be seen, we went to the dockyard where we were shown through by a policeman.*
>
> *On the 22* [**Wednesday**] *I went to Torcross with Misses E. Jeffery, M. J. & C. Cranch, Mr E. S. Bickford & J. Wills.*
>
> **Friday 24th July 1863:** *in the afternoon went to South Sands in Steamer. Explored the cavern in the rocks near there with candles, then had a walk on the Bolt Head.*

As in London, so back in Devon, it is striking how very mobile people seem to have been. Many of these young people must have been cousins, for they all seem to have been the children of the Kingsbridge business community, which was heavily intermarried[68]. (How they were all able to take so much time off in the working day is less clear!) A closer analysis of that

---

[67] http://genuki.cs.ncl.ac.uk/DEV/Stokenham/Logbook.pdf.
[68] Lidstone 1989.

business community would no doubt reveal a more stratified structure – and might identify the Paines as on one of the lower rungs.

On a higher rung were the Gards. The girl Charles cared most about then, one senses, (though five years later she married someone else), was nineteen-year-old Tillie Gard, the sister of Charlotte, of whom he had seen a good deal in London. Matilda Harriet Gard ('M. H. G.') was the daughter of James Gard, tailor and mercer of Duke Street. Years later someone pencilled below her photo in his album 'V. great friend of CCP!'

Clara Cranch, a Kingsbridge friend.
Photo: J. Ash, Kingsbridge.

A fortnight before he left for London Charles had joined a Gard family trip to Torcross, a local beauty spot – indeed he had paid 7s to hire the Britzka carriage. From London he sent her a letter, a 'portrait', a Christmas card and a Valentine, but no sooner was he back in Kingsbridge than Tillie took off on a six-week holiday. She went with her eldest sister Elizabeth Fuller and family from Plymouth, to stay at Little Ash Farm at South Brent, a large village on the railway line twelve miles north of Kingsbridge. Charles visited them there, and arranged a date to visit the Bath and West of England Show[69] at Exeter. Everything that could go wrong with that trip seems to have gone wrong; were Charles and Tillie able to see the funny side?

Matilda ('Tillie') Gard, born 1844, Charles's 'v. great friend.' This must be the photo for which Charles paid Mr Ash 1/6d on August 24th 1862 – though it has lost the mica he bought with it.
Photo: Ash, Kingsbridge.

11th June 1863: *S. Perrot called me about 4-15. I got down, had a cup of tea with him, after which we went to the Kings Arms Hotel, from whence we started at 5-40 in Foal's break, himself driving, in company with Mr. Willcox & Son, Mr. Gillard, Mr. Burge, Mr. Badcock and Mr. Parhouse* [sic: ?Parkhouse] *& Son. We thought the weather was fine, but before we reached Loddiswell we had showers. We arrived at K. B.* [Kingsbridge Road] *Station about 7-25 and as it was raining I was afraid M. H. G. would not come down from Brent, I not then knowing that the Excursion train stopped there. I therefore took the first train to Brent, walked to Ash Farm* [about half a mile out of the village] *met her coming out, left the cakes I brought over for Mrs Fuller, and returned to Brent Station as fast as I could with Tillie, where I took 2 first Class returns to Exeter where we arrived between 10 & 11 am. Proceeded up High Street (saw the Guildhall, an ancient looking place) to the Queen's Hotel, Queen Street, where we had luncheon. (It now again commenced to rain). We took Buss to the Agricultural Show which we entered about 12, it is all*

---

[69] see *Trewman's Exeter Flying Post* June 17 1863.

enclosed in a boarded fence about 10 feet high in a nice level field, but owing to the quantity of rain that has fallen the former part of the week and the amount of travelling over the ground, the front of entrance was one pool of mud ankle deep; but inside it was not quite as bad. We went through the various departments, some of which did not much interest me; there were two very nice conservatories there, in which were a few nice flowers. There was also a large tent erected, in which there were many beautiful and rare plants, with a fountain playing in their midst. On the opposite side was the Fine Arts Gallery, or rather tent, in which were placed a number of paintings by local artists, both in oil & colour, a few of which were good, also works of art & skill in great variety, both Modern & Ancient, a few of the ancient cases being brought from the Kensington Museum. We next walked round and saw the Cattle and Machinery, from thence to the Poultry tents where there was a good show of the feathered tribes. We then passed on by the Agricultural Implements (and saw a great many other articles too numerous but well worthy of mention,) to the refreshment tent amidst heavy rain where, after taking a refresher in the shape of tea and buns, and waiting nearly 2 hours for the rain to cease, we sallied forth into it. On our way out it was a complete pool all through the field, and at the entrance it was much worse than when we came in. After trying in vain for a bus or cab, we waddled through the slush, to the Horticultural and Dog Show, the rain all the time pouring down in torrents, even dripping through the canvas. The Flowers in this department were splendid, as were also the fruits and vegetables. The dogs I only took a summary glance at, it being in an awful dirty state, on account of the rain, which was then pouring through the roof as through a sieve. After seeing all that we could, as well as the state of the weather would permit, we made our exit from the grounds and took a cab for the station (for which we had to pay dear) [3/-], where we arrived about 6 pm[70]. After waiting about an hour and quarter we again started for home; left Tillie at Brent and

---

[70] So the trip took six hours each way; Charles seems to accept that as entirely normal.

Louisa ('Louie') Bickford, born 1844, William Bickford's sister. Photo: Barnes & Son, Mile End Road, London.

arrived at Kingsbridge Road about 10 (I saw there H. Mitchelmore) and arrived home about 12 O'clock.

Five weeks later Charles went with her father to fetch Tillie home:

21st June 1863: *Dined at Mr Gard's on roast duck. After dinner I drove Mr Gard and Miss L. Bickford* [Louisa, William's younger sister] *to Brent on a visit to Mrs Fuller and M.H.G; had tea at Little Ash Farm where they are staying... M.H.G returned home with us. There was a misty rain descending which made us wet.*

Little Ash Farm, South Brent, Devon, in 2013. Photo: Crispin Paine.

What happened later

On November 22nd Charles, back again in London, wrote what he clearly expected to be his last letter to his father:

> I am very sorry to hear by every account I receive from home, that you still remain so very unwell. I was in hopes when I left, that you would soon be able to get about again, and that you would be spared to us some time longer, but if it be the will of the Lord to remove you from among us, I trust what will be our loss, will be for your gain. I am anxiously looking forward to coming home at Christmas, to which time I hope we shall all be spared to meet together...

He writes of plans to buy a house, and possibly move his sister to London, and promises to take care of her and the children. In fact his father did hang on until Christmas, dying on New Year's Eve.

At that time Charles was in partnership with Henry Oldrey, but two years later with George Jordain. About 1865 Jordain and Paine did a deal with the Tyssen-Amhurst estate in Kingsland, and by 1866 were already

Gravestone of William Paine, Charles's father, in West Alvington churchyard, in 2013. Photo: Crispin Paine.

Colvestone Crescent, Dalston, in 2013. Charles came to live in the newly-built No. 17 when he returned to London, and Jordain & Paine had their office there; the present-day No. 17 is on the left. Colvestone Crescent leads into Ridley Road, famous in the 1940s for local Jews' resistance to the fascists, and now for its multi-ethnic market, immortalised in EastEnders. Photo: Crispin Paine.

laying out new streets around St Mark's Church. They built 120 houses in Sandringham Road that year, and many of the houses in Colvestone Crescent; this substantial number made them one of London's larger house-builders[71]. This is LB Hackney's St Marks Conservation Area, 'notable for the excellent survival of high quality middle-class Victorian housing.'[72]

Charles moved his sister and her children to London and installed them round the corner from the Colvestone Crescent

---

[71] LB Hackney 2008; Hunter 1981, 16.
[72] LB Hackney 2008, 7.

house where he was living with the Jordain family, and where the Jordain and Paine business was based. The firm developed St Mark's Rise in 1867, and were still building in Alvington Crescent (named after Charles's father's birthplace) in 1876[73].

The Hackney Gazette carried an advertisement on 31st May 1871:

> HOUSES – St. Mark's Square, Down's Park, and Sandringham-road – within 5 minutes walk of Dalston junction, containing from 7 to 12 rooms. Fitted with hot and cold water baths, Venetian blinds, gas, bells, and every other convenience. Large rooms, good gardens, with back entrance and convenience for Stable in the rear – portion of the purchase money can remain if required. Apply to Jordain and Paine, 17, Colvestone Crescent, Ridleyroad.[74]

At the end of September 1871 Charles married his partner's sister Ann, and two children quickly followed, Charles Albert in 1872 and Annie Elizabeth in 1874. The following year George Jordain died, but by then Charles and Ann were well established, and they moved to their first substantial house in 1876 – five years later they were employing a cook, a governess, a nursemaid and a housemaid.

When Charles Paine died aged 90 in 1932, he had ten children and fifteen grandchildren. He had been a Master of the Worshipful Company of Wheelwrights and an Alderman of the City of London, he lived in a substantial Georgian house in Hampstead, and he had an (entirely spurious) crest on his silverware.

---

[73] LB Hackney 2008, 30.
[74] Reproduced in Hunter 1981, 22.

SOURCES AND ACKNOWLEDGEMENTS

The diary is a small 16mo notebook of ruled and lined pages in a leather cover with a cover flap – very much a pocket-book. Charles used it for a number of different things:

- the diary itself, which he wrote almost every day.
- petty-cash accounts from August 1862 to June 1863.
- addresses, both (a few) friends, but also addresses of shops ('Rimmels Perfumed Valentines'), often roughly noted in pencil rather than in the elegant copperplate ink of the rest of the notebook.
- lists of letters written and received.
- a couple of pages of (awful) riddles and their answers ('Why is the letter K like a pig's tail? Because it's the end of Pork').
- Extracts from the will of Mary Cleverly, his grandmother.
- 1861 census figures for various South Devon towns and villages, and for London (he gives 1,679 for Kingsbridge and 1,302 for Dodbrooke).
- recipes to harden iron, restore faded ink, cure chilblains, and a 'French recipe' for Baked Mutton Chops.
- 'Facts and Scraps', including the legend of St Swithin, facts about coins and how to waterproof boots.
- the meaning of some Christian names.
- 'Account of work to be done at No. 18 Clifton Gardens.'

I have very gently edited the diary entries, merely adding punctuation and correcting a few misspellings. I have not pursued Charles beyond the dates of his diary, despite the survival of his petty cash book for 1864 and 1865.

Sadly, the only business record of Jordain and Paine that seems to survive is a rent roll book for the firm's last two decades, 1941-1962, now in Hackney Archives. However, the firm followed a very similar trajectory to that set up by another South Devon boy who came to London in the early 1860s, C. A. Daw and Son Ltd., whose business archive survives from 1875[75]. By the end of the century Jordain and Paine, like Daw and Son, had become property managers rather than any longer builders[76].

I have used other sources besides the secondary ones referenced below:

- Charles's photograph album. Most of the photos (all but one of them of individuals, and almost all cartes-de-visite) seem to have been taken in the 1870s, and sadly few have their names pencilled in below. The cream of those that have are reproduced in this book.
- A petty-cash book kept by Charles from September 1863 to December 1865.

---

[75] Belcher 1982, 25

[76] Isobel Watson comments: 'I think this was a common trajectory among those few builders who kept some or most of their stock in hand, as opposed to selling it on. Others who did so were John Grover and Sons, James Hartnoll, and the Davis brothers. But these were rare: most builders seem to have exhausted the available land in an area, sold all the stock and moved on.'

- *Notes from the life of a doctor's wife in Victorian days from year 1876 to the year 1970*, a MS booklet by Charles's eldest daughter Edith Pritchard (1876-1975).
- *The Paine family*, a typescript by Michael Paine, 1982.
- The Paine family tree. This was mostly originally researched between the wars by Charles's fifth daughter, Janet.
- The Paine family photograph collection.

Charles seldom uses first names, and to identify 'Miss E. Crimp' or 'J. Bennett' can be a challenge. I have mostly used the censuses to track them down, accessed via ancestry.co.uk, together with White's Devon Directories of 1850 and 1878-9, and Billings's Devon Directory of 1857. Though I cannot guarantee them, I am reasonably confident that I have correctly identified most people. To identify London streets I have used Stanford's 1863 Map of London, reprinted by Old House Books, and the Ordnance Survey 1871-2 25 inch maps, reprinted by Alan Godfrey.

At Kingsbridge, I am most grateful to Ann Lidstone of Kingsbridge History Society for her encouragement, correction and invaluable advice, and for sharing with me some of her extraordinary knowledge of the Lidstone family and of the town's wider history. I must thank for their help and guidance the staff and volunteers at the Cookworthy Museum, especially in its excellent Research Room, and for a number of bright ideas Kathy Gee, sometime curator there.

In London I am especially grateful to Isobel Watson, who not only gave generously of her time to discuss a variety of points major and minor, but helped me begin to understand London as a Londoner might, and London history as a London historian might. I must thank, too, the staff of Westminster City Archive, London Metropolitan Archive, and Pam Czerniewska (a great-granddaughter of Charles) for her greatly helpful advice and encouragement.

Without access to London's various university libraries a study like this would scarcely be possible, so I am ever indebted to UCL's Institute of Archaeology which makes it so. And one ought, too, to acknowledge Google, without whom it would take impossibly long.

Afterword

This short study has barely scratched the surface of some of the issues Charles Paine's diary touches on. In Kingsbridge, it would be very good to see an analysis of the town's social structure in the middle of the nineteenth century. Such a study would throw light on southern English society more generally. Kingsbridge deserves, too, a study of the movement of its children away, similar to that which L. C. Williams (2002) has carried out for Marlborough in Wiltshire.

What was the impact of the migration of these young skilled people from the South West to London and further afield – on social consciousness, as well as on wages and business organisation? Charles's story suggests that skilled provincial workers had been brought up to see themselves as middle class rather than working class. A related area that seems to cry out for more examination is the adult education movement, and the social and political impact of the 'Reading Rooms'[77].

In London it would be good to see much more analysis of the mid-Victorian building trade, and the role of small firms like Jordain and Paine, in different parts of the metropolis. A further study of the development of Hackney, to go alongside Isobel Watson's admirable 1989 study of South Hackney, and to build on LB Hackney's *St Marks Conservation Area Appraisal*, would also be very valuable.

---

[77] There is a useful bibliography in Cherrington 2012.

References

Devon

Bickford, James, 1890. *James Bickford: an autobiography of Christian labour in the West Indies, Demerara, Victoria, New South Wales, and South Australia 1838-1888*. London: Charles H. Kelly. Available at http://archive.org/stream/jamesbickfordaut00bick#page/2/mode/2up.

Born, Anne and Tanner, Kathy, 1986. *Kingsbridge Devon*. Kingsbridge: Kathy Tanner.

Fox, Sarah Prideaux, 1874. *Kingsbridge and its surroundings*. Plymouth: G. P. Friend. Available at www.archive.org/stream/kingsbridgeitssu00foxs/kingsbridgeitssu00foxs_djvu.txt, and on iTunes.

Hoskins, W. G., 1954. *Devon*. A new survey of England. London: Collins.

Lidstone, Hugh R. G., 1989. *Lidstone of the South Hams*. Kingsbridge: Lidstone Family History Society.

Pitman, A. J., 1872. Fly-fishing adventure with an alligator. *The South Australian Advertiser*, 10 June 1872. Available at: http://trove.nla.gov.au/ndp/del/article/28686122.

Saville, John, 1998 [1957]. *Rural depopulation in England and Wales, 1851-1951*. Abingdon: Routledge.

London

Anson, Peter F., 1960. *Fashions in church furnishing, 1840-1940*. London: Faith Press.

Belcher, Victor, 1982. The records of a London building firm. *Business Archives* 48.

Borman, William, 1868. *The life of the ingenious agricultural labourer, James Anderton, the founder and builder of the model of Lincoln Cathedral, as shown in the Exhibition, London, 1862, made from one million eight hundred old bottle corks.* Newcastle: J. Beall.

Burton, Anthony, 1999. *Vision and accident: the story of the Victoria and Albert Museum.* London: V&A Publications.

Cherrington, Ruth, 2012. *Not just beer and bingo: a social history of working men's clubs.* Bloomington, IN: AuthorHouse.

Dyos, H. J., 1968. The speculative builders and developers of Victorian London. *Victorian Studies* 11, supplement: Symposium on the Victorian City (2), Summer.

Gänzi, Kurt, 2002. *Lydia Thompson: queen of burlesque.* Abingdon: Routledge.

LB Hackney, 2008. *St Marks Conservation Area appraisal.* London: LB Hackney. Available at www.hackney.gov.uk/ep-conservation-st-marks.htm#.Ur74tijGfvY.

Hobhouse, Hermione, 1995. *Thomas Cubitt: master builder.* 2nd edn. London: Mercury Business Books.

Howell, Peter and Sutton, Ian, 1989. *The Faber guide to Victorian churches.* London: Faber & Faber.

Hunter, Michael, 1981. *The Victorian villas of Hackney.* London: The Hackney Society.

Hyde, Ralph, 1988. *'Panoramania'.* London: Trefoil Publications and Barbican Art Gallery.

The Morning Chronicle: Labour and the Poor, 1849-50; Henry Mayhew – Letter LX.

Morton, William H., 1905. *Sixty years' stage service, being a record of the life of Charles Morton, the father of the halls.* London: Gale and Polden.

Munby, Arthur Joseph, 1972. *Munby, man of two worlds: the life and diaries of Arthur J. Munby, 1828-1910.* London: Gambit.

Postgate, R.W., 1923. *The builders' history.* London: National Federation of Building Trade Operatives.

Powell, Christopher, 2nd edn. 1996. *The British building industry since 1800: an economic history.* London: E. & F. N. Spon.

Ritchie, James E., 1858. *The British building industry since 1800: an economic history.* London: E. & F.N. Spon.

Rose, Walter, 1937. *The village carpenter.* Cambridge: Cambridge University Press.

Satoh, Akira, 1995. *Building in Britain: the origins of a modern industry.* Aldershot: Scolar Press.

Skyring's Builders Prices, 54th edition, 1864. London: Skyring. Available at: http://books.google.co.uk/books?id=ww8FAAAAQAAJ&pg=PA108&dq=skyring&hl=en&sa=X&ei=xTmKUYDXIMGh0QW874DwBw&ved=0CDUQ6AEwAQ

Summerson, John, 1973. *The London building world of the eighteen-sixties.* London: Thames and Hudson.

Timbs, John, 1867. *Curiosities of London: exhibiting the most rare and remarkable objects of interest in the metropolis, with nearly fifty years' personal recollections.* London: David Bogue.

The Victoria County History of Middlesex Vol 10, 1989. Oxford: OUP.

Watson, Isobel, 1989. *Gentlemen in the building line: the development of South Hackney.* London: Padfield.

White, Jerry, 2007. *London in the nineteenth century.* London: Jonathan Cape.

Whitehead, J., 2001. *The growth of St. Marylebone and Paddington.* London: privately published.

Wilkinson, Anne, 2000. Stoke Newington and 'the Golden Flower'. *Hackney History* 5.

Williams, I. L., 2002. Migration and the 1881 census index: a Wiltshire example. *Local Population Studies* 69, Autumn.

INDEX

Page numbers in italics denote illustrations. Page numbers followed by an 'n' refer to footnotes on that page. The extracts from the diary given in this book have not been indexed.

Alhambra Music Hall 7, 46, 47
Alvington Crescent 79
"American Cousin, The" 48
architects
   Burton, Decimus 49
   Butterfield, William 60, 60n
   Cundy, Thomas 60
Australia 24, 26, 27

Barnes, Arthur 46-47
Bath and West of England Show 74-75
Battersea 31, 41
Bendall's Dancing Academy 51
Bennett, John 23, 39
Bennett, Thomas 23
Bickford, Edmund 24
Bickford, Louisa 76, *76*
Bickford, William 23, 24, 33, 45, 46, 60, *76*
Bignell, Henry 25
Blondin 39, *40*
"Bluff King Hal" 48
British Museum 1, 39
British Oak Pub 10

Brooke, Gustavus Vaughan 48
buses 33, *34*

Caldwell's Dancing Academy 51
Canterbury Music Hall 46
churches 60-61, 70, 78
City of London Theatre, Bishopsgate 48
Clifton Gardens, No. 18, work at *15*, 16, 18n, 80
Colosseum, Regents Park 49-50
Colvestone Crescent, Dalston 78, *78*, 79
Covent Garden 48
Cranch, Clara *73*
Crimp, E. (Emma?) 70, 82
Crystal Palace 39, *40*, 51

Damerell, John and Maria 29
dancing 51
diary 1, 6-7, 9, 14, 16, 22, 31, 33, 51-53, 59, 62, 66, 80-81, 84

Ellis, Jane Lome (aunt) 69

Flower Pot bus terminus 33
Foale, Charlie 23, *23*, 40, 51, 54, 62
Forces Tavern, Blackawton 3, 65, *65*
Fore Street, Kingsbridge 3, 24, 66, 70, *71*

Gard, Matilda H. (Tillie) 73, 76
Great London Exposition (International Exhibition) 1862 36, *37*
Greenwich 41
Greville House Working Men's Library and Reading Room 55-58

Hackney 12, 33, 78-79, 78-79n, 81, 84
Hampstead 79
Hannaford, Henry 25
"Henry VII" 48
Hill, Susan 28, 68, *68*
Holy Trinity Church 60
house building boom 8, 11-12
Hyde Park 30, 61

Independent Church, Kingsbridge 60-61
International Exhibition (Great London Exposition) 1862 36, *37*

Jordain, Ann (wife) 3, 79
Jordain, George 3, 25, *25*, 77, 79
Jordain and Paine 77, *78*, 79, 81, 84

Kellond, Henry (Kelland) 16, 16n, 18
Kellond, John 16n
Kingsbridge 1-2, 2n, 66, *71*, 80, 82, 84

Lakey, George 29
Langworthy, Joseph 25
Little Ash Farm, South Brent 73, 76
"Little Goody Two Shoes" 48
Lloyd, Arthur 47
"Love's Triumph" 48

Mackney, E. W. 46-47
Marx, Karl 1, 39
Mayhew, Henry 12-13, 15, 19, 61
Moysey, Sarah 32
Metropolitan Underground Railway 33, 35, *35*
migration of country carpenters to London 8, 27, 84
Mill Street, Kingsbridge 66, 70
Music Hall 7, 31, 45, *45*, 46-47, 50

Notting Hill fair 53

Oddfellows Fete 70
Oldrey, Ann 3, 46, 48
Oldrey, Henry Baker 3, 16, 19, 45-46, 48, 77
Oldrey, Sarah 3
Oldrey, Jane 3, 64, 65
Oxford Music Hall 45, *45*

Paddington Green 55
Paddington Station 4, 33, *64*
Paine, Annie Elizabeth (daughter) 79
Paine, Charles frontispiece 3, *52*, 52-63
  apprenticeship 1, 18, 20
  books 21, 58
  children 79
  clothing 53
  correspondence and presents 28, 58, 64, 68
  crest 79
  finances/savings 59
  gardening 53-54
  in Devon 64-76
  leisure 30-51
  meals 54-55
  politics 61-63
  titles
    Alderman of the City of London 79
    Master of the Worshipful Company of Wheelwrights 79
    President of Stoke Newington Chrysanthemum Society 53
  religion 59-61
  social status 53
  work 10-21
    tools 20, 20n, 21
Paine, Charles Albert (son) 79

Paine, Charles Frederick (half-nephew) *67*
Paine, Clarenda (Clara) (half-niece) *67*
Paine, Edith (daughter) 52, 82
Paine, Elizabeth (nee Allinson) (grandmother) 27
Paine, John (grandfather) 27
Paine, John (uncle) and Mary (step-aunt) 68
Paine, Mary (half-sister) 3, 28, 64, 66, *67*, 70
Paine, William Henry (father) 3, *3*, 59, 64, 66, 68, 77, *77*
Peek, Richard 27-28
Pepper's Ghost illusion 50-51
Perrott's Saddlery Shop 70, 70n, *71*
Plymouth 69, 69n, 70
Polytechnic 50
Port, William 53

Randolph Road, No. 7, work at 7, 16, *17*, 18
Redhill 45
Reeves, Sims 40
Regents Park 31
Richmond Road 19, *19*, 20n
Robinson, Frank 28
royalty 38, *38*, 41-44, *43*, 50-51, 55
runaway apprentices 22, 28

St Germains Terrace, No. 3, Paddington 3-5, *5*

St Mark's Conservation Area, Hackney 78-79
St Mark's Rise, Hackney 79
St Matthias Church 60
Salcombe 2, 2n, 39
Sandringham Road 78-79
Sawyers, Louisa 25, 44
Sawyers, W and L (William and Louisa) 25
Sinkins, Charles H 27
Society of Arts 56-57
Sothern, Edward Askew 48
South Hams people in London 22-29, 33n
South Kensington Museum 38-39, *38*
Spurgeon, Charles 61
Sunday Closing Bill 62

Templeton's African Opera Troupe 69
theatre 48
Thompson, Lydia 48
Tildesley, David 16
Torcross 72-73
trade unions 58-63
Trameer, Thomas Brockwell 39
Tucker, Edward 25
Tucker, Matilda (Tillie) 25, *26*
Turnhams Music Hall 46
Tyssen-Amhurst Estate, Kingsland 77

underground railway 33, 35, *35*, 48-49
Unsworth, James 46-47

wages 11n, 13, 15, 59
Way, Mr 19-20, *19*
Weekes, Adela 4n, 8, 24, 31, *64*
Weekes, Rosa 18, 24, 55
Weekes, S and W 18
Weekes, Samuel (elder) 3, 8, 18
Westbourne Park Crescent 3-4, *5*
Westons Music Hall 47
Widger, Burnett 24-25
Windsor 44-45
women, social rules 31-38
working men's clubs 55-58
Wills, Edwin 32, 32n
Wills, William 32n, 68, 70
West Alvington 27, 29, 68, 77